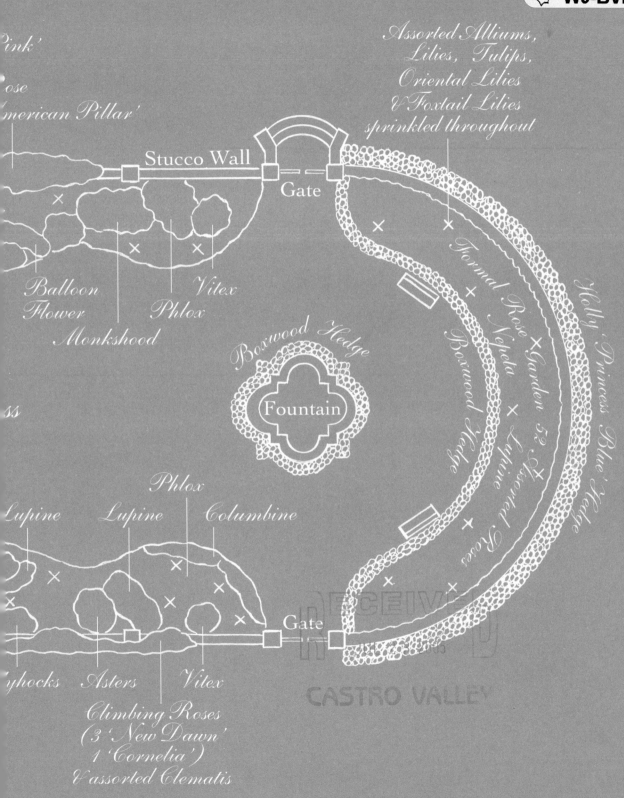

'Pink'

'ose

'merican Pillar'

Stucco Wall

Gate

Assorted Alliums,
Lilies, Tulips,
Oriental Lilies
& Foxtail Lilies
sprinkled throughout

Balloon
Flower

Phlox

Vitex

Monkshood

Boxwood Hedge

Fountain

'Formal Rose'

Nepeta

Boxwood Hedge

Garden 52 Assorted Roses

Lupine

Assorted Roses

'Holly' Princess Blue' Hedge

ss

Phlox

Columbine

Lupine

Lupine

Asters

Vitex

yhocks

Climbing Roses
(3 'New Dawn'
1 'Cornelia')
& assorted Clematis

Gate

CASTRO VALLEY

Suzy Bales' down-to-earth GARDENER

Suzy Bales'
down-to-earth
GARDENER

LET NATURE GUIDE YOU TO SUCCESS IN YOUR GARDEN

Photographs by Richard Warren

RODALE

Portions of this book have previously appeared in different form in *Newsday* and *Family Circle* magazines.

The information in this book has been carefully researched, and all efforts have been made to ensure accuracy. Rodale Inc. assumes no responsibility for any injuries suffered or for damages or losses incurred during the use of or as a result of following this information. It is important to study all directions carefully before taking any action based on the information and advice presented in this book. When using any commercial product, always read and follow label directions. Where trade names are used, no discrimination is intended and no endorsement by Rodale Inc. is implied.

Printed in China
Rodale Inc. makes every effort to use acid-free ♾, recycled ♻ paper

Book design by Doug Turshen
Illustrations by Rodica Prato

Photos of *Rosa* 'Heritage' on page 126 and *Rosa* 'Golden Celebration' and *Rosa* 'Mary Rose' on page 127 are courtesy of David Austin Roses, Albrighton, Wolverhampton, England

We're always happy to hear from you.
For questions or comments concerning the editorial content of this book, please write to:
Rodale Book Readers' Service
33 East Minor Street
Emmaus, PA 18098

Look for other Rodale books wherever books are sold. Or call us at (800) 848-4735.

For more information about Rodale magazines and books, visit us at **www.rodale.com**

Library of Congress Cataloging-in-Publication Data

Bales, Suzanne Frutig.
    Suzy Bales' down-to-earth gardener: let nature guide you to success in your garden / Suzy Bales.
           p.   cm.
    Includes bibliographical references and index.
    ISBN 0–87596–894–5 hardcover
    1. Gardening.   I. Title: Down-to-earth gardener.   II. Title.
    SB453.B333   2004
    635—dc22   2004010038

Distributed to the trade by Holtzbrinck Publishers

1 2 3 4 5 6 7 8 9 10 hardcover

RODALE
LIVE YOUR WHOLE LIFE™

OPPOSITE: Teddy, the family pet, dozes among the blue wood geraniums, forget-me-nots, and azaleas blooming along the woodland walk.

to my sister,
Jayne Mengel

a down-to-earth approach to gardening

It is a universal truth that plants talk and gardeners are notoriously poor listeners. I should know—I was a poor listener. Plants are honest creatures, incapable of concealment. They speak their mind through their body language. Simply put, flowers that bloom their heads off, eagerly reseed, run in all directions, and grow robustly tell the gardener they are happy. A drooping stem, a hanging head, a ghostly color, and a limp leaf are a few of the ways a plant expresses its unhappiness. When satisfied, gladioli shout, sunflowers laugh, mums murmur, and cyclamen whisper. Roses sing hallelujah, and I listen with rapt attention.

Perfection is not possible, nor is perfection what a garden is about. It is about change that is driven by the cycles of the seasons and the aging of the plants. No living thing is perfect. Even plants catch cold, get depressed, and die untimely deaths. Many go through periods when they are not attractive; like pimples on the young, this soon passes. Each gardener must decide if the plant can be loved regardless of its faults. With many of my favorite plants, like some of my friends, I've learned when to look the other way.

Like most of us, plants can be temperamental. They can be cajoled, humored, and even dressed up, but if their basic needs are not met, they perform in a lackluster way. It is useless to try to force an unhappy plant to behave. It's far better to learn how to please it or, if it is too demanding, exchange it for another. The better you know your plants, the easier it is to play to their good points and ignore their bad. No living thing is without flaws (except perhaps one's own children).

OPPOSITE: Once the ivy on the front of the house skipped under the porch, it swagged the ceiling and softened the cold stucco, turning the porch into a restful green grotto.

No matter how much you read and study the principles of gardening, the real learning comes from planting, tending, and watching the plants themselves. Plants behave differently in different environments, and thus each garden is unique. And many garden myths are just that—fallacies passed along from gardener to gardener that do nothing but mislead.

Once I began questioning conventional garden wisdom and turned to my own garden for the truth, gardening became more fun, and I became a much better gardener. The garden provides a learning curve, prodding the gardener onward and upward. What happens there often turns conventional book learning on its head (although there *are* some excellent books—for a list of my favorites, turn to "Bibliography" on page 196). Don't be stifled by worrying how to do what when. It can curdle your spirit.

Tending a garden has left me in awe of nature's ways. It is there that I am closest to God. Everywhere I look, I see miracles of birth, growth, and change. Moments of breathtaking beauty often catch me by surprise. Every hour I spend in the garden, I learn something new, yet at the close of each garden year, I am filled with more questions than answers. There is so much more lurking under the surface, just beyond our immediate grasp. We can't accurately predict tomorrow's weather, let alone next season's bloom. Knowing this instills respect, awe, and awareness that there is a divine plan.

The yellow Darwin hybrid tulips my husband planted on our sandy beach have returned each year for 25 years.

The Garden's Mysteries

In the normal course of my gardening, I have experienced many strange and wondrous events. A daffodil drops a seed through a crack in the retaining wall. It sprouts and blooms. I couldn't reach in and remove the bulb if I wanted to. Giant sunflowers do the same in the stone courtyard. (How the seed travels from the kitchen garden to the courtyard is anyone's guess.) Branches of ornamental cherries, crab apples, and vitex poked in the ground to stake plants take root and sprout foliage. Under an azalea, a peony grows where I never planted one.

Or mutations appear. The variegated 'Gold Heart' ivy sprouts a stem with all-gold leaves. When I see it, I snip it—it provides an especially nice touch of gilt in a floral arrangement. Although I don't understand why, the variegated porcelain vine reverts to solid green if not cut back to the ground every few years. I act accordingly.

After heavy rains, I discover colorful mushrooms and giant puffballs, which appear—poof!—like magic. I'm positive they weren't there the day before. The unexpected joy of discovery is exhilarating.

Every day the garden reveals new secrets, things I never read about in books. I've learned that the description of a plant, whether in a book or on a nursery tag, is scarcely more than a rough guide to the plant's usual behavior. Often such descriptions, such as the size or length of bloom, are misleading, and sometimes they are blatantly wrong. The same plant in a different place or under different circumstances might be a freak or a goddess, a giant or a midget. I have grown a 6-foot bearded iris and an 8-foot monkshood. (Experts flatly state that bearded iris grows to 40 inches and monkshood to 4 feet. Neither of mine was fed with chemical fertilizer nor planted on top of a cow plop.)

'Gold Heart' ivy occasionally sprouts a stem of solid gold leaves. It makes a nice swag on a basket of English roses and columbine.

Most plants can grow in a wide range of conditions. When my husband planted a dozen yellow Darwin hybrid tulips on our sandy beach 25 years ago, I laughed at him. I pointed out that if the occasional saltwater bath didn't kill them, the lack of nutrients in the soil would. The tulips on the beach have returned each year for 25 years. (The ones I planted in rich garden soil were gone after a season or two.) So 3 years ago, we turned the sandy strip of land where the woods run onto the beach into a tulip cutting garden. Sometimes it takes a while for us to catch on.

Indomitable Mother Nature

A garden never belongs wholly to the gardener. Although the gardener plays a part in its health, Mother Nature's mood and whims dominate. She's no saint. She can by turns be benevolent or pugnacious—sometimes in the same day. At the turn of the 21st century, winter's inevitable last gasp covered us with several inches of snow on April 9, following a day of sunbathing amid balmy temperatures in the 70s. In less than 18 hours, temperatures plunged 40 degrees, and rain turned to whooshing gusts of snow. Plants that could normally withstand low temperatures were caught off guard; with their soft new shoots exposed, they up and died.

In the course of a year, the same garden can be calm, colorful, orderly, and messy. It can stop me in my tracks one moment and be ho-hum the next. More-

For a garden to thrive, a gardener, like a seamstress, has to specialize in alterations.

over, no two years are alike. Because of a prolonged drought in 2002, fall hardly happened, while the fall before was one of the longest and most colorful in recent memory. Nothing stays the same—what performs beautifully in a rainy, cool summer may well sulk in a dry, hot one. For a garden to thrive, a gardener, like a seamstress, has to specialize in alterations.

In more than 30 years of gardening, I have never finished a garden. There have been times when I thought I'd gotten it just right. Then new inspiration and challenges flowed from conversations over the garden gate. A garden is a continuing story, bookmarked somewhere in the middle.

In a garden there will always be failure, death, and disease. But there will also be celebration, joy, glory, and heart-wrenching beauty.

My purpose in writing this book is to help you seek out the truths of your own garden, to question everything, and to enjoy and appreciate the everyday miracles you'll find there. There will be many.

Where I Garden
What I know about gardening is firmly rooted in our 6-acre property. The garden is based upon heavy clay soil, USDA Plant Hardiness Zone 7 temperatures, salty sea breezes, and my passion for flowers. In many ways, it is my autobiography. In the first summers, while I rocked my babies to sleep and read them books in the hammock on the side porch, I envisioned flower borders in the side lawn with a rose garden in the distance. It was many years before these became a reality. Moreover, as I planted one garden, ideas for two or three more came to mind. This is still going on, with no prospect of completion.

My gardening began as a private passion. I was a closet gardener for many years until visitors and neighbors started spreading the word about what I was up to. Despite the pleasure my garden may have given to others, gardening is very much a personal addiction. Many of my garden methods developed from the need to balance caring for my family with tending plants. Garden chores had to be stripped down to the essentials. No weekly attention could be given to my flower gardens—even less to the lawn, which I admit is poorly kept. When time was scarce in the early years, I learned how to work more effectively in partnership with Mother Nature to exploit what happens naturally. It turned out to be the best way to learn. But as the kids have grown up and left home, gardening has occupied me more and more. I don't waste much time trying to please every plant, which is impossible anyway. I choose my plants as I choose my close friends—easygoing, hardworking, kind to others, uncomplaining, happy with their situation in life. You will find plants that meet these requirements again and again in different beds, in different combinations.

Having flowers to pick for the house is one of the best gifts from the garden.

The garden is growing up gracefully and learning to care for itself (so are the kids, in case you're wondering). Many of the foolish endeavors of our youth together have faded from memory, and new ideas, more sensible and better grounded, have taken over. This is the story I want to tell.

A LOOK BACK   In 1978 my husband, Carter, and I purchased a piece of property on an island off the north shore of Long Island. The Tudor house had been well built in 1908, but it had languished along with its reclusive owner in the 40 years before we purchased it. Not a bit of paint or polish had touched the inside. Outside, heavy swags of honeysuckle and ivy covered the walls and even the windows—scarcely a gleam of sunlight entered and then only through peepholes clipped (apparently with nail scissors) by the late owner. Prospective buyers scurried away; the idea of living in a haunted house was too much for most people. It had been on the market for years when we saw it. Luckily for us, the seller had finally chopped the ivy and honeysuckle to the ground before we arrived or we, too, might have turned and run. Instead, we found the house warm and welcoming, each room flooded with sunlight as had been originally intended.

The grounds were equally neglected but had once been well planted. Century-old pin oaks lined the circle driveway and reached out to embrace the front lawn. There were no foundation plantings around any of the buildings—the main house, carriage house, boat barn, and storage shed. An old, decaying apple orchard was slowly expiring next to the south porch, and a woodland of brambles, tulip trees, and ivy—both poison and English—roamed to the north. A large kitchen garden, fenced in with chicken wire, was hidden from the house. We moved in late in December and the following year discovered how few flowers had survived the neglect—snowdrops, iris, a climbing rose, and a wild rose or two. But there was a patch of autumn crocus (*Crocus speciosus*). The crocus, probably planted when the house

Autumn crocus blooms in the woods as hosta shows its fall colors.

and the lady were young, had naturalized in the woods. It was a wonderful gift that I've come to appreciate more and more over time. Autumn crocus is so rarely planted in American gardens. As the bulbs increased in numbers, I have scooped up clumps and transplanted new colonies in distant corners of the woods.

During the early years, we spent most of our time, money, and energy fixing up the interior of the house. The balance shifted gradually to the outside. I began by planting wildflowers, shade perennials, and spring bulbs at the top of the woodland walk.

Next, I sowed the kitchen garden with cutting flowers, vegetables, and herbs. I still had no idea how addicting gardening could be, nor how joyful and satisfying. I only knew it made me happy to have flowers and vegetables to pick.

OUR PLAN In the early 1980s, we engaged Alice Recknagel Ireys, a prominent landscape architect, to design a comprehensive plan for our property. Her first comment was shocking. Catching a glimpse of a recently planted azalea and hosta bed, she exclaimed, "It looks like a motel planting. Take it out!" As so often happened afterward, she was right. We had combined the loudest colors of azaleas: neon orange, flaming red, royal purple, and flamingo pink. For years afterward, Carter planted only white ones.

Alice was one of those rare people who are outspoken and opinionated yet never offensive. She instilled trust and respect. Our relationship started with her working for us; it evolved into me working for her. I drove her to her clients' gardens, hauled plants around, placed them before they were planted, edited two of her books, and took photographs for one; all the while, she taught me the importance of designing with nature while paying attention to the classic principles of scale, proportion, unity, balance, and rhythm. A garden must not look contrived or too planned but as if it came into being on its site as an act of nature. That's not to say she disapproved of major alterations, such as changing the slope of the land or adding a stream and a pond or two. It is just that the result should not *appear* man-made. Each of the thousand or so gardens she designed fits its site and looks as if it has always been there.

Alice Recknagel Ireys, an extraordinary landscape architect, always dressed in a suit when working on a job.

The plan she designed for us divided our property into several different garden rooms with different purposes. A formal perennial and crescent-shaped rose garden replaced the dying apple orchard. A lilac and peony walk connected it to the kitchen garden. A small orchard of a dozen fruit trees was planted inside a living fence of espaliered apples and pears at the entrance of the property. At the back of the house, Alice tucked a small pond. It emptied into a stream that wound down the hill before tumbling over a waterfall into a larger pond where a pump returned the water back up to the small pond through an underground pipe. Years later, she designed a swimming pool and tennis court. Finally, a dozen years ago, she had us turn the carriage yard into a courtyard paved with large flagstones, with plantings of herbs, bulbs, and groundcovers between the stones.

FAMILY CONTRIBUTIONS Of course, we didn't create all of these gardens on our own. We hired help for the bigger projects and have had a full-time gardener, Manuel Castillo, for 15 years. My whole family has been involved in one way or another.

The goldfish and frogs in the small pond at the back of the house entertain Teddy endlessly.

My husband, Carter, it must be said, is the most accommodating of men. For the most part, he admires the beauty of the gardens and encourages me to plant more. He never questions my garden expenses, feeling blessed that my passion is flowers rather than jewels. In the early years, Carter placed and planted dozens of azaleas and rhododendrons in the woods and along our property line. He even transplanted six forsythia from dozens along the driveway to the back of the woods despite my protests that they wouldn't have enough sun. The forsythia proved to be adaptable, blooming slightly less but in a softer, more pleasing yellow.

Lately, Carter is spending time designing a new gazebo and turning a storage building into a garden shed. Not quite an armchair gardener, he occasionally ventures out with pruner in hand. He also takes the matter of weeds in the gravel driveway very seriously, asking Manuel to spend a half-hour a day removing them. (I, naturally, discourage this practice. It is simpler to run them over with the car or park over the weediest spots, especially during a rainstorm, thereby desiccating them.) The ivy on the house is another of his chosen gardening chores. He watches it keenly and insists that it be kept off the porch, the windows, and the roof, conspiring with Manuel to trim it back when I am out running errands. Last summer I announced that the ivy creeping under the porch ceiling was not to be touched—on pain of death. Somehow they obeyed, and it has covered the ceiling and turned the porch into a green grotto.

My mother loves to weed, but never where I think it's needed. Whenever she visits, she sets her cushion among the clover in the lawn, selecting the spot with the best view of the bay, and commences to remove all the greenery within reach, leaving a bare spot that needs replanting in the heat of summer.

My daughters save me a great deal of time deadheading. They both love to pick flowers, and when they leave with armfuls, there is less for me to do. My sons, too, have hit on an efficient way of pruning the shrubs and roses around the basketball court. Hurling a ball can snap off so many branches in such a short time.

I had no idea how addicting gardening could be, nor how joyful and satisfying.

Our West Highland terrier, Teddy, joins the family fun. Besides his uncanny modeling career (wherever I aim my camera, he is front and center), he roots rodents out of the kitchen compost. When he runs circles around the bin, I know it's time to dump leaves on top of the vegetable clippings. I keep a garbage can of leaves nearby for that purpose. He is also a personal trainer. He runs the resident gray squirrels across the lawn and up trees, and he leads me in stretching exercises every time we stand up.

However, most of the time I work alone. Gardening is my solitary pleasure. And because I do most of the work, I make most of the decisions about moving plants and adding and subtracting as I see fit. I even take credit for beautiful combinations that happen by accident, and no one is the wiser.

rules for a down-to-earth approach to gardening

When I began gardening, I followed all the rules. Today I make my own rules—and break most of the existing ones, as well as my own. Questioning what's taken for granted is part of the fun. Here are the rules I've embraced.

- For the greatest impact, garden up!
- Plants die. Accept it!
- Just say no to chemicals.
- When in doubt, sow alyssum.
- If you don't know it, don't pull it.
- Unless you want to be a weekly weeder, don't leave bare soil.

- Plant more bulbs—the easiest path from rags to riches.
- Allow plants three strikes before they're out.
- Learn when to fight, when to turn your head, and when to accept defeat.
- A shady spot is an opportunity for a soothing garden.
- When designing a garden, pay no attention to a plant's classification.
- When something needs doing, just do it.
- Wise gardeners grow common flowers.

- Don't follow plant fads.
- A gardener's thumb is only brown when soil clings.
- Trial and error is the best teacher.
- Each plant does not need its own square footage.
- Let plants lean, hug, and climb on each other.
- Pruning is a sometime thing.
- Make time to enjoy the garden.
- You can rationalize anything.
- Occasionally, bring in the clowns.
- Never take yourself too seriously.
- Throw out the rules!

In midwinter, the green noses of fragrant Solomon's seal (*Polygonatum odoratum* 'Variegatum') break through the ground and I know that spring can't be far behind.

the delights of weeding

self-seeders

the essentials

putting the garden to bed,
or just letting it doze off

The Delights of Weeding

Speaking as a gardener, I don't think you can get much more down-to-earth than weeding. My weeding has never been planned and deliberate. I don't wake up and say, "Today I'll weed the kitchen garden," nor

Foxgloves, lupines, and sweet Williams reseed freely in the back bed of the kitchen garden and are transplanted elsewhere.

do I choose a day in advance on a calendar. Weeding is usually spontaneous.

I start off walking through the garden to see what's in bloom, to check which seeds have germinated, to water, and so on. Before I know it, I'm sidetracked into weeding. Dealing with weeds is like eating potato chips: You can never pull just one. Sometimes an hour passes before I'm vertical once more and back on the path I started out on.

When walking through the garden with friends, I may absentmindedly pluck a weed or two and toss them under the nearest shrub to decompose. Nongardeners find this quite shocking, but that's nature's way. After a major cleanup, most weeds end up in the compost pile. If they are about to go to seed, I dump them in the trash.

friends who don't garden can't accept the idea that I am enjoying myself when I'm weeding. The myth that it's drudgery, an unpleasant chore, is too much with us. Truth be told, weeding is a stolen pleasure, time all to myself. The monotonous rhythm of repeated action allows my mind to wander—my imagination unclogs, and the frustrations of daily life are washed away with the glow of perspiration.

My pleasure in weeding increases after a soaking rain, when even onion grass, dock, bindweed, lamb's-quarters, shepherd's purse, and chrysanthemum weed, all my most tenacious weeds, can be pulled out whole from the soft ground without a trowel. If it's warm enough, I like to weed in a gentle rain.

As my mind drifts, my eye records what is happening in the garden. Often I end up sitting or sprawling at the edge of a border to avoid stepping into the bed and compressing the soil. Reaching in and under the plants, I've found myself in positions that might tax a circus contortionist. But by bending down, kneeling, squatting, or even lying on the ground, you can get such an intimate view of the world of plants.

There is much to be learned, but not all of it is pleasant. A streak of silvery slime on the ground or over a leaf tells me slugs have taken up residence. Squelching slugs

is a great sport, but not for the squeamish. If I weren't at ground level, I might not have noticed what was afoot until huge chunks were missing from the leaves. Or I might spot a scurry of sow bugs, one of the garden's beneficial decomposers, usually a sign of a decaying plant nearby. What lurks in the shadows is often the clue to solving a plant mystery or catching a destructive culprit before the damage is done.

More often, however, this close-in approach opens windows into the wonders of the garden. Peering at the innocent, brightly colored, intricately designed, and seemingly expectant faces of **violets** and their many relatives, I am in awe of the handiwork of Mother Nature. She never seems to repeat herself.

Some tenacious weeds with roots that run, skip, and jump. FROM LEFT TO RIGHT: *Petasites japonicus*, poison ivy, artemesia, *Houttuynia cordata*, and gooseneck loosestrife.

I grew native North American violets for decades before I noticed last September tiny nodding purple buds under their heart-shaped leaves, an inch or two above the ground. I kept an eye on them all fall, thinking that perhaps they had been nudged by summer drought to bloom out of season, but they never did. Trying to find an answer, I consulted the perennials expert, Dr. Allan Armitage. He explained that true violets produce two different kinds of flowers. The showy spring flowers I love to pick are infertile. Consequently, later in the season, another set of flowers that never open form at the base of the plant. They are known as *cleistogamous* flowers, and their sole purpose is to self-pollinate within the closed bud and to form seeds. These flowers have the ability to spew their small seeds up to 9 feet from the plant. Checking back under the leaves later in fall, I found the dried, open seed capsules.

If You Don't Know It, Don't Pull It

Weeding can be a treasure hunt as well as a simple cleanup. Learning to identify seedlings is a necessity if we hope to accept nature's gifts. In any case, exercise care. If I don't know it, I don't pull it. It's a gamble to let it grow, yet I often get lucky. (It's my idea of living dangerously.) Of course, I first check to see if the mystery seedling is part of a group found in only one part of the garden. If it is, the probability is high that the mother plant is nearby. If it's a lonely specimen, it could have been dropped by a bird, carried in with the mulch, floated in on a breeze and parachuted down, or unknowingly smuggled in on the back of our dog. But if it's a weed, chances are that others like it will be scattered widely. Still, appearances can be deceiving: Remember that the first leaves on a brand-new plant are cotyledons, not true leaves, so wait until the true leaves

a garden vignette

I admit to planting 'Heavenly Blue' morning glory every year. The offspring revert to small flowers in different colors, which are actually pretty enough to warrant leaving a few. I might as well; I honestly couldn't weed them all out if I tried. They are sneaky devils, twining around other plants, hiding from view until they bloom, and then it's too late—I am, yet again, entrapped by a pretty face.

are evident before making a positive identification.

In a garden, new seedlings appear daily. Some are showy: The red leaves of amaranth give it away. Some are gawky: A tulip tree seedling has tulip-shaped leaves too big for its britches. Some are ferny: Nigella, a miniature of its mother, is all aflutter in a light breeze. And some are instantly identifiable: Lupine, for example, has its foliage arranged in tight whorls. Once I learned to recognize my favorites, I let them be or scoop them up and move them to a better spot. Extras are always welcome gifts to neighbors and friends.

Morning glories would, if they could, take over the earth. Besides their glorious good looks, I grow them so curious children can pinch their puffed buds and hear them pop. Each flower blooms for only a day before it literally goes to seed. 'Heavenly Blue', a hybrid, drops hundreds of seeds over the course of its 3- to 4-month bloom by my estimation. Even if I wanted to, I couldn't wipe out the entire population with one swipe because the seeds don't germinate all at one time; they keep coming all summer and fall.

Verbena bonariensis blooms with musk mallow (*Malva moschata*).

Flowers of Discontent

heading my list of unwelcome plants are the "flowers of discontent" that wander at will and stomp on everything in their way. We thoughtlessly introduced many of these, not taking the time to check their credentials. **Spirea**, for example, has taken over the path and driveway garden. The **musk mallow** (*Malva moschata*) has skipped to and fro across the length of the formal border. **Gooseneck loosestrife**'s cocked head is scanning the woods, planning its advance. Clumps of **purple loosestrife**, the roadside menace, have suddenly appeared—two in the perennial garden, one in the meadow, and another at the top of the bank. This means all-out war.

Nursery salespeople and catalogs can be deafeningly silent about a plant's true habit. To be fair, a plant's behavior may depend greatly on where it is planted. **Lady's mantle** has been known for her promiscuity in other gardens, but in mine she is a lady—too much so, unfortunately. Her chartreuse locks are one of my favorites for poking into bouquets of roses. And I love the way she cradles raindrops in her leaves, where they delicately glisten like pearls in the sun.

Unfortunately, I've come to love many invasive perennials. I want to keep a few of each around, and that's the rub. With some of them, it's all or nothing. I know I have to pull up the excess spirea, musk mallow, and gooseneck loosestrife in spring. Others simply need to be placed in a correctional facility. Mint minds its manners if confined to a pot. Chives, too, must be imprisoned for life. The real troublemakers—purple loosestrife and creeping liriope come to mind—have to be yanked out by their feet and tossed in the garbage if we are to have anything else in the garden.

Underground Discoveries

Weeding takes me underground, into the secret lives of plants. How else would I know about colorful roots? It is not something that you normally find in books. Ask most anyone, and they will likely say, "Roots are brown, silly."

The chartreuse flowers of lady's mantle enhance almost all other flower colors, whether in a garden or a bouquet.

When in bloom, **gooseneck loosestrife** is a quiet beauty with a gracefully arching head covered in altar-boy white starry flowers. Such looks are deceiving. Its true color shows underground, where you find scarlet roots that are the devil to dislodge. They run in all directions, sometimes several feet, before rearing into an angelic-looking plant. If the soil is moist and loamy, I can apply a slow, gentle pressure and pull out a foot or two at a time. If the soil is dry and crusted, Lord help me. I bring out the spading fork, employ brute strength, and begin the lifting. The only line of defense is hard work—or a cement barrier. I must warn you against dividing gooseneck strife regularly to keep it in check, as many garden writers recommend. Dividing it only helps it multiply. Luckily, the red runners are easy to spot when they come up for air in spring. The red at the base of a small plant's stem is the signal for gardeners to take warning.

The bright white roots of **creeping liriope** (*Liriope spicata*) defy conventional wisdom. I made a big mistake by planting creeping liriope one time. Every family has its saints and sinners, and this one is a sinner. Conversely, cultivars of *L. muscari* are so well behaved you can take them anywhere. They slowly increase without an inclination to conquer. They are also better-looking, with wider leaves and showier flowers. I unfortunately let the creepy liriope, as I call it, roam far too long and cover too much ground. I will be removing it for years to come. Thankfully,

Truth be told, weeding is a stolen pleasure, time all to myself.

the bright white runners are easy to spot—how do they stay so white romping in all that dirt?—but they are so plentiful that it's easy to miss a few. This is why, when weeding out a menace such as this one, I always revisit the area weekly to yank up new shoots.

If you see any of these pesky perennials growing in a friend's garden, I suggest that you dart in and pull them out without wasting a minute.

Self-Seeders

Mother Nature is Lady Bountiful to those who work *with* her; Cruella De Vil to those who don't. She freely gives gifts of seedlings, knowing which ones flourish. At times our tastes clash—a normal parent-child relationship. When we agree, I'm blessed.

In the kitchen garden, both clary sage and leeks flower and scatter seed in their second summer for the following year's blooms.

When I let her **have her way,** the garden almost cares for itself. **As I age,** our relationship has grown deeper, **more loving,** and more respectful.

I've learned not to be too quick to deadhead flowers. "Let the seeds fall where they may" is my motto, at least until I get to know a plant's habits. Self-sowing plants may be charming or exasperating, but they're almost always unpredictable. Sometimes I've found new hybrids, especially among the hellebores and columbines. Sometimes a hybrid—a morning glory, for example—drops a seed that reverts back to a species.

I welcome self-seeders, some might say foolishly, with open arms; they save time, money, and energy. Tomatoes, lupines, foxgloves, sweet William, love-in-a-mist, hellebores, clary sage, black-eyed Susans, and forget-me-nots are a few of the plants I never have enough of, even though they freely give of themselves. I can always squeeze another seedling into one of my gardens.

However, sorting out Mother Nature's gifts in their many guises takes practice and a discerning eye to distinguish a weed from a desirable plant. Once I began letting them have their way, flowers bloomed where I hadn't thought it possible—pansies in the gravel driveway, sunflowers between the paving stones, forget-me-nots (the most cooperative of all) anywhere they touch the earth.

You can rationalize anything!

Cleome, planted the summer before, reseeded among the tomatoes; I let some stay and transplanted others.

Embracing Annual Reseeders

One friend has called me a permissive gardener. And it is true. I like to see what a plant is going to do before I start pushing it around. Sometimes I already know.

Last summer I spied some **tomato** seedlings under a hedge of roses planted to hide the trash bin. No one goes near it unless they are emptying the trash, and I can cut rose blooms from it to my heart's content, with no concern about damaging a garden ensemble. The tomato seeds had lurked in the compost I emptied under the roses. Out of the compost emerged a plum tomato plant, a currant tomato plant, and a cherry tomato plant—an excellent kitchen garden selection. The roses embraced the tomatoes as they grew and supported the tomato vines until they reached more than 5 feet—nature's own tomato cage! These self-seeded tomatoes began ripening the second week of September, when the kitchen garden tomatoes were finishing, so I was able to pick tomatoes and roses together for the dinner table. An admirable partnership.

Often the places that tomatoes germinate are better suited to their needs than the places I choose. I assume they move around the beds with the help of the fat rodents—perish the thought—that leave half-eaten tomatoes here and there. Per-

I like to see what a plant is going to do before I start pushing it around.

haps it's the work of my friends the birds. As a rule, tomatoes are not relished by critters, but I have found a half-eaten green tomato balanced on the railing of the playhouse; I suspect it was deposited there by a gray squirrel that frequents that spot. Other plants sprout where tomatoes fall off the vine and rot. Seeds can, and often do, stay in the soil for many months or even years before they germinate.

In the kitchen garden, I rely heavily on flowers that reseed. I'll religiously deadhead the dahlias to encourage more bloom, but rarely do I deadhead the annuals. Last year **cleome** seeded itself between the tomato cages at one end of the row and the amaranth at the other. Because the tomato leaves are often blemished, ragged, and disheveled by the time I pick the fruit, the cleome was a welcome camouflage and a distraction from the tomatoes' scruffiness.

Snow-on-the-mountain (*Euphorbia marginata*) is an annual I haven't planted for years. Last summer, one plant showed up unannounced. I must have brought up a dormant seed, deeply buried a few years ago, during spring planting. (I am reminded of the fields of red poppies that bloomed across northern France and Belgium at the end of World War I. The skirmishes of war disturbed their sleep, and their poignant return symbolized the blood that was shed.) I love the beauty of its soft green leaves unevenly outlined in white, as if painted by the hand of a child. Still, you have to take care with snow-on-the-mountain. Growing it is easy, but it can be troublesome when snipped for flower arrangements. Poisonous white sap oozes out and may cause a skin rash similar to that of poison ivy. The sap flow can be stopped by dipping the cut stem briefly in boiling water or searing it with a match. Otherwise, sap can clog the stems of the other flowers in the arrangement and prevent water absorption. I have been handling snow-on-the-mountain for years and luckily have never had a problem. (However, if I merely *look* at poison ivy, I start to itch.)

a garden vignette

A few years ago, I was digging out a lupine for transplanting when a toad leaped from under its roots. Toads, it turns out, are fond of covering themselves with soil. After I recovered my breath, I welcomed him. Toads are a blessing in a garden. They find insects a gustatory delight. But I'd appreciate a little warning first.

Clary sage (*Salvia sclarea*) is a controversial member of the salvia family. It is loved from afar for its beauty but can be a stinker—literally—up close. Its odor is antiseptic (the best that can be said for it), but its beauty is arresting. As far as I am concerned, it is welcome to roam the kitchen garden, where, as a hardy biennial, it blooms early in its second year. The showy, inch-long translucent flowers are softly tinted with pink and purple tones. They bloom in whorls around the 3- to 4-foot stems. When I spy clary sage seedlings, I might move them to the formal garden for their glory days, then pull them up when their leaves start to rust. *(continued on page 18)*

Love-in-a-mist (*Nigella damascena*) quickly blooms from seed. Sometimes it reseeds and blooms three times in a year.

Love-in-a-puff
(*Cardiospermum halicacabum*)

Hellebore
(*Helleborus* × *hybridus*)

Foxglove
(*Digitalis purpurea*)

Sweet William
(*Dianthus barbatus*)

Black-eyed Susan
(*Rudbeckia hirta*)

Blue lupine
(*Lupinus perennis*)

Snow-on-the-mountain
(*Euphorbia marginata*)

Forget-me-nots
(*Myosotis sylvatica*)

There is nothing controversial about **love-in-a-mist** (*Nigella damascena*). It is a sprinter. In less than 2 months from sowing, it blooms its head off. The cornflower blue flowers open amid a feathery green boa of foliage. As the flowers are finishing, the seedpods puff up to the size of Tootsie Roll pops, lightly sponged with reddish brown spots. After flowering, it drops its seed as if to embroider the earth. One long summer it self-seeded and bloomed three times in the same spot. Another year, it was caught half-grown by snow and simply sat tight until spring before sprouting another few inches and blooming. Not a hair on its pretty head was damaged or blackened by the frost.

Perennial Self-Seeders

Perennials don't readily self-seed in the formal garden. Over winter, I dump compost on their heads to enrich the soil and feed the community (I've learned that perennials won't thrive without it). And in summer I don't leave bare spots. As a result, seeds don't have much chance to germinate and grow. Most clumping plants, like balloon flower, monkshood, and garden phlox, increase slowly underground anyway.

But in the early years, I was distressed that the foxgloves and lupines kept dying out. One summer, to be safe, I collected ripe seeds from the **foxgloves** (*Digitalis*) and immediately sowed them in the kitchen garden. Luckily, due to a cluttered mind and an overambitious to-do list, I didn't move all the resulting seedlings into the formal garden next spring as I had planned. The few plants left behind in the kitchen garden readily seeded themselves. Now I purposely leave a few there each spring to produce a new crop of seedlings.

a garden vignette

When I was in my teens, my first boyfriend brought me a bouquet of **black-eyed Susans**. He said they reminded him of me. I was insulted; I thought of myself as a rose. Many decades later, I've changed my mind. I find myself drawn to the simplicity of daisies for the very reasons I rejected them in my youth. Daisies are joyful, fun-loving, unassuming, and easygoing. I admire their disarming innocence, their humility, and their defiance of life itself. In the wilder reaches of our grounds, the black-eyed Susans' yellow faces bring sunshine and light.

The Russell hybrid lupines (*Lupinus*) initially planted in the formal garden bloomed lushly for only a year or two before dying out. I kept replacing them with new plants (a costly process) until I decided to try the native blue lupine (*L. perennis*) from seed. I now prefer its fragrant blue spikes to the red, pink, and blue mixture of the hybrid. I seeded a clump of native blues in the back bed of the kitchen garden, hoping they, too, would self-seed, and they turned out to be very generous.

Almost as prolific as morning glories, the hellebores (*Helleborus*) in the woodland garden often produce a dozen seedlings in a 6-inch square, usually under their mother's skirt. The covering protects them from being smothered by my yearly fling of compost or shredded leaves. Only a few plants would survive the struggle for space on their own. I have close to 100 percent survival among those I transplant. The first year I potted up the seedlings and carefully nursed them through summer. The pointlessness of this coddling became apparent the next year when, being short of time, I simply transplanted 2-inch seedlings straight into other areas of the woodland garden.

Forget-me-nots start blooming with daffodils, stay to greet tulips, and then leave when roses dominate the show.

To start with, I planted three species of hellebores—*H. niger, H. foetidus,* and *H. orientalis.* Because they intermarry with abandon, I now have a garden of *H.* × *hybridus* seedlings that flower in muted colors from pink to deep purple. I never know what I'm going to find. To retain pure colors, the varieties must be kept separate; because I don't separate them, I have a natural crossbreeding lab. Just think! I might make a new discovery—that recurring gardener's dream.

Black-eyed Susans (*Rudbeckia hirta*) take self-seeding insouciance one step farther. They couldn't care less whether they get sun or shade, moist or dry soil, hot or cold summers. Their seedlings tend to stick close together but are not reluctant to spread. They originally let themselves in at the sunny entrance to our woodland walk and have since marched right into the shade. They seeded themselves into the ivy that grows densely by the pool and thrived in the clay in our sunny meadow, where many a wildflower has bit the dust.

Forget-me-nots (*Myosotis sylvatica*) bloom with the early daffodils and wave good-bye to the last tulips. Their blue flowers don't compete for attention with

the daffodils and tulips but enhance their beauty. In late June, when forget-me-nots go to seed, their stems blacken, and the tops of the plants look dead. Because there are so many seeds clinging to dead stems, I simply pitch the cut stems into a tarp or garden bag, scattering them later directly into the garden between late-blooming perennials and anywhere I want a new crop for next spring. There's no need to pick off the seeds. I've started forget-me-nots growing everywhere I plant bulbs, around the base of trees on the front lawn, under shrubs, and at the highest points along the woodland walk, knowing they will work their way down as they self-seed during subsequent summers.

MOTHER NATURE'S NURSERY

Without planning it, the back bed in the kitchen garden has become my self-perpetuating nursery. Sweet William, clary sage, foxgloves, lupine, love-in-a-mist, and others wander in and live their lives with little interference from me. I snatch up their seedlings and use them to replenish the other gardens. I might weed here once or twice a year, but mostly they have to hold their own against each other. They happily reseed in their allotted space as well as drift into the wood-chip paths and occasionally into the nearby beds. I am grateful for their progeny and let them wander where they will.

Shrubs and Trees That Self-Seed

It is not just annuals and perennials that reliably self-seed. Shrubs and tree seedlings are easy to find, too, if you know what to look for. Under a rose-of-Sharon, I counted more than six dozen babies. Anybody want one? They're so plentiful that I attack them with a hoe.

Juniper seedlings don't come in large numbers. But they seem to seek out the most difficult terrain to grow in. For years, a juniper seedling has been standing smack against the trunk of a century-old pin oak, squeezed between the large roots. It's only 1½ feet tall and stopped growing years ago. It is a natural bonsai. Although it doesn't belong there, I admire its tenacity, so I leave it and point it out to visitors.

The cutest of all, a baby crape myrtle, sprouted a few yards from its mother. It was a wee thing, less than a foot high and covered head to toe in flowers. It is a good thing I never got around to making its bed before it bloomed, or I might have mistakenly weeded it out!

OPPOSITE: In late June, the back bed of the kitchen garden is Mother Nature's nursery where lupine, foxgloves, sweet William, and clary sage—among others— bloom and reseed yearly.

Collecting seed

Flowers make everyone feel better, and they make me happy. So to have more, I took to collecting seed, especially of plants that need no coddling to bloom. Old-fashioned favorites top the list—nigella, forget-me-nots, sunflowers, poppies, lupine, and foxgloves. I don't collect seeds from hybrids because their descendants revert to their parental varieties, usually very different and often less attractive. I purchase these new each year.

What I didn't anticipate was how collecting seed would open windows into the private lives of plants, giving me a look at the intimate details of their existence. Along the way, I became a more successful gardener.

Seeds, of course, come in all sizes, from the coconut to the finely ground "black pepper" of nicotiana or the even smaller begonia seeds that can be counted only under a microscope. Seeds also come in different colors and patterns—some spotted, others streaked.

Love-in-a-puff (*Cardiospermum halicacabum*) captured the attention of Catie, my youngest child. A delicate vine with small green leaves and tiny, pinhead-size white flowers, it isn't much to look at early on. The magic is in the seedpods—round, papery puffs, 3 inches across, hanging like green Ping-Pong balls. When they turn brown, they pop like small balloons—and here is the best part—revealing three round, black seeds, each marked with its own perfect white heart. When I excitedly showed them to Catie, she predictably just said, "Mom, please, I've got to go," and raced off to be with her friends. It wasn't until the next day that I discovered the vine had been completely stripped of every puff, most not even ripe. As soon as I turned my back, Catie had brought the whole neighborhood to pop the puffs and collect the seeds. I'm not usually lucky enough to get such quick results from trying to teach my children anything. The vine took it in stride, chugging along all summer like the little engine that could, continuously producing new flowers and puffs.

I get a particular kick from nature's trigger-happy seedpods, the ones that explode to the touch when ripe. Even if you're not saving the seeds, triggering an explosion brings out the child in us all. **Cleome** and **impatiens** are two that blast off when the time is right.

Marigold seeds are among the easiest to collect. They present themselves in tight bundles held aloft as if praying, "pick me, pick me." The seeds slip easily out of the pod into your hand.

Columbines (*Aquilegia*) hold their seeds upright in tulip-shaped pods. I pick the pods and shake them along the woodland walk where they love to grow. No special care is needed to help them along. Given 3 or 4 months to grow before heavy frost, they bloom the following spring.

The spiky seedpods of **angel's trumpets** (*Datura*) are the size of golf balls—and look as menacing as a medieval mace. The pods split when ripe, and black seeds spill out. They so readily reseed that I never have to collect the seeds unless I want to give them away. I just move the seedlings to new places each spring.

Who doesn't remember making a wish as a child before blowing the gauzy puffs of dandelions? **Japanese anemones** (*Anemone × hybrida*) are the adult version. Standing taller and thus easier to reach than dandelions, they readily respond to a breath of air. After the flowers fade, small green buttons stand upright in their place. When the seed is ripe, the wind opens the buttons to reveal fluffy balls of cotton peppered with tiny seeds. These are blown apart and float away over the next few weeks.

The pods of **poppies** (*Papaver*) are nature's pepper shakers. When the wind sways the pod, the tiny black

seeds spill out into the garden. **Nigella** seeds, clunkers in comparison, are also housed in round pods. They crack as they age to release the seed. Smashing the crusty pods of poppies and nigella to collect the seeds sometimes gives me pause. Although I want to collect the seeds for next year's flowers, I also like to save the pods for dried arrangements. Compromise is necessary.

Not so for **sunflower seeds.** I ruthlessly chop off the ripe round heads and hang them inside the garden shed where the seeds can continue to ripen without being eaten by birds. I once did as suggested in a gardening book, placing paper bags over the heads and tying them tightly with ribbons. But this looked so ridiculous that I couldn't bear it. Even drawing faces on the bags to add a little whimsy didn't help. I had to

Shirley poppies can be sown as soon as the snow melts. Late frosts won't hurt them.

remove them before the week was out.

Usually when I collect seeds to save over winter, I take plastic sandwich bags along with me to the garden. Each seed variety has its own separate bag with a handwritten label inside. When collecting smaller seeds, I hold the bag open under the pod when I snap it off. I put the bag over the pods when collecting trigger-happy seeds. I handpick larger seeds and place them in the bag. But most important (I learned the hard way), before sealing the bag, make absolutely sure that the seeds are dry; otherwise, they will rot. Store the seeds over winter in a cool, dry place such as the door of a refrigerator.

Collecting seeds offers rewards beyond providing flowers for my garden and for friends. It keeps me moving. Otherwise, I, too, might go to seed.

Putting the Garden to Bed, or Just Letting It Doze Off

In my Zone 7 garden, where snow comes and goes and a few warm days are sprinkled throughout winter, I never put my garden to bed. Admittedly, it dozes off, but rarely does it sleep deeply.

If not deadheaded, the dried flowers of mop-head hydrangea hang on all winter, even if frozen in ice sculptures.

25

In my early years of gardening, the more garden books I read, the more work I thought I had to do.

In the rose garden, I corseted the roses in burlap to protect them from the cold, even though they grew in a protected spot in front of a holly hedge. After the first frost, I obediently cut all of the perennials to the ground, covered the perennial bed in salt hay, pulled up the annuals, and gathered the fallen leaves. I was so happy to see the garden season end that I collapsed in front of the fire for the next few months, rarely venturing a walk through the garden.

By spring, fully recovered and raring to go, I uncovered the perennials and re-moved the burlap, undoing everything I had done in fall. It took me years to un-derstand the wastefulness of all this labor. Most of the plants were perfectly able to handle the cold without my help.

In those early years, I did too much too soon. I know now the wisdom of leaving annuals untouched in fall. Many of them survive early frost and con-tinue to bloom longer into winter than might be expected. A first frost is often followed by an extended Indian summer, when many annuals recover to bloom yet again. Some half-hardy souls—snapdragons, for instance—have been known to live clear through a mild winter, with only a few days of snow cover here and there, and then bloom their heads off the following spring and summer. Pineapple sage and Mexican sage both die back to the ground but may well send up new shoots from their roots in late spring if given a chance.

The dried stalks and flowers of perennials add to the beauty of winter, whether they are bitten by frost, glazed by ice, or dressed in snowy gowns. Astilbe, sedum 'Autumn Joy,' and ornamental grasses are a few of my favorites. I love the bronze fall color of peony foliage, and I don't remove it until it is definitely unsightly, often not until midwinter.

Autumn is when dawdling is not a downfall. These days I clean up the dead fo-liage and fallen leaves as the spirit moves me. Even planting bulbs can be a leisurely

undertaking, starting in September and ending in early December before the ground freezes.

In fall, the peony foliage turns to bronze as the trees are changing colors.

When it comes to fallen leaves, I know too many people who are foolishly tidy. They insist on removing them, bagging them, and hauling them away to the town dump. Whenever I pass leaves piled on the curb, I have the nearly uncontrollable urge to take them home. Leaves are one of the greatest gifts nature gives us. The soil needs replenishing each year with organic matter, and the natural source of such matter is the leaves dropped by trees and shrubs. The leaves decompose into humus, which contains the nutrients plants need, as well as the roughage to make the soil friable and well structured. Humus is my garden's gold. I never have enough. It is to the garden what milk is to a baby—a complete and nutritious food. It improves the aeration of the soil and absorbs, retains, and then slowly releases moisture. I find it extraordinary that something so easily obtained is not more highly valued. Mother Nature has made it too easy.

Compost It!

Compost happens! And I let it! It's a major miracle in nature's grand scheme. And miracle is the only word to explain how rotting garbage and leaves become fine black velvet humus, rich in sustenance. It is so clean that it protects plants from diseases, parasites, and toxins. It is a medicine for worn-out soils, an elixir for healthy ones. A good dose of humus can raise a soil's water-holding capacity from only 20 percent of its dry weight to between 300 and 500 percent. Peat moss, itself a particular type of humus, can absorb from 600 to 1,200 percent moisture on a dry weight basis. It is easy to see that the more moisture a soil can hold without becoming soggy, the better plants grow in it.

Mistakenly, many gardeners believe that it is sufficient to add a chemical fertilizer. A chemical fertilizer does add nutrients, but it does no good for the soil structure, and over time the soil compacts, preventing the nutrients from reaching the roots of plants. Yearly replenishment of the soil with humus is the single most important step in building a garden. I rarely use fertilizer. I admit that I've occasionally spread cow manure on the formal garden and an organic fertilizer around my roses, but this is a holdover from reading too many books and seeing too many fertilizer ads. I never notice a difference in growth whether I fertilize or not.

A pile of leaves takes from 6 weeks to 6 months—or more—to turn into rich, black compost, depending on the height of the pile, the amount of rainfall, and the temperature. Composting is not simply a fall activity. I have ongoing piles in two large wooden bins filled with leaves, long grass clippings (it is best to leave short clippings on the lawn, where they will automatically rot and enrich the grass), and other dead foliage and plants gathered over the entire year.

Wood ashes from the fireplaces are added to the mix, although I caution you to be sure they are cool enough to hold in your hand before you empty them onto the pile.

I keep a plastic compost bin by the kitchen door for kitchen debris, layering it with leaves or grass clippings to speed up the change and to keep out rodents. In the corner of the kitchen garden, another plastic bin takes weeds and trimmings

a garden vignette

Someone tossed smoldering wood ashes on our dried leaves once. They erupted in the early morning into a four-alarm fire. We were away at the time, but an alert night watchman at the yacht club across the bay called the fire department. The fire was out before it caused too much damage, although the force of the fire hoses dug trenches and holes throughout the garden. Incidentally, it also distributed the ashes far and wide, into places where afterward plants grew more lushly than ever before or since.

from the cleanup of that garden. Although there are many ways to make compost faster, I take a lazy approach: I simply pile up the material and let it work at its own pace.

After the big fall rake-up, we shred about half of the leaves and return them immediately to the beds. The rest go in the compost pile. Shredded leaves make attractive mulch, break down quickly, and refresh the soil. If you don't have a shredder, a lawn mower can be pushed back and forth over a pile of leaves with the same result. The danger of leaving whole leaves on the grass or in beds is that they tend to compact and prevent water from getting into the soil. In the wilder parts of our property—behind the tennis court, at the back of the woods, and in the tangle of shrubs and wild roses that separates the driveway from the lilac and peony walk—I let them be. These places will never be tidy. They serve as shelters for the birds and animals and are not, in fact, unsightly. The foliage is so dense that during most of the year visitors walk right by and never notice the disorder.

Dried flower heads of sedum 'Autumn Joy' are decorative capped in snow.

The Wonders Never Stop

fall is also a time to gather the last rosebuds and enjoy them indoors or dry them for winter bouquets. The tiny wonders of a fall garden—the scarlet, orange, and golden rose hips, the frost on a rosebud, perhaps a lonely flower blooming during the first snowfall, warmed by the skirts of another—deserve more attention than they get. I can almost always find a confused flower—generally a lilac, viburnum, or forsythia—blooming as late as November.

Walking in the garden on a sunny winter day is a pleasure. After heavy frost and a snowfall, the dried perennial stems and foliage are brittle and snap off at a touch. Sometimes I put on big boots and play Godzilla, stomping over the frozen bed, snapping off the dead perennial foliage. It is a lot quicker and more fun than bending over and cutting them off in fall. If I leave them until late winter, they fall over on their own, and I collect them for the compost heap. They are always welcome there.

the kitchen garden

the woodland walk

the gardens

the formal flower garden

the formal rose garden

the flagstone courtyard

the lilac and peony walk

the shinking lawn

gardening up

Peony 'Festiva Maxima',
with its white feathery petals
flecked with scarlet, dates
from 1851, yet it is still one
of the best varieties.

The Kitchen Garden

Our kitchen garden is a wonderful mélange of flowers, vegetables, and herbs. As it was the first garden I planted, it was intended to complement a house filled to overflowing with family and guests each summer,

By October in the kitchen garden, nasturtiums cover the path, Mexican sage is in full bloom, and morning glories join the woolly morning glory at the top of the arbor. The scarecrow watches over the garden but doesn't keep the birds away.

so a mixture was inevitable. Not much was planned and logical about it.

In truth, we stumbled, hesitated, and backtracked even as we raced forward creating it. A garden of this sort encourages experimentation and imagination because it need not be beautiful, only productive. Missteps are not as obvious as they might be in a perennial border. But making it taught us a great deal that we put to use later. We learned to observe more closely what the plants themselves wanted to do, to encourage them to self-seed, and to allow one clump of flowers to softly weave into another. Most important, we learned that if we don't know a plant, we don't pull it until it identifies itself.

The existing kitchen garden was a large rectangular plot framed by chicken wire when we arrived. We went to work immediately. First, we outlined a circular area for herbs, creating a herringbone path of old bricks that lead in from the gate. We laid the bricks on the inside of the path on end, which allowed topsoil and compost to be heaped 8 inches higher than ground level. This improved the drainage.

We divided the circular bed into four sections and planted it with the basic culinary herbs and in the following years added another half-dozen basils, assorted scented geraniums, and decorative salvia, including pineapple sage and Mexican sage, which we wouldn't be without today. Wanting more color among the greens, we dressed the center with four 'Simplicity' rosebushes and massed ruffles of alyssum and lavender at their feet. The roses were chosen for their strong constitution. No chemical sprays have ever been allowed in the kitchen garden.

A dozen years later, it seemed a shame that the roses in the herb garden lacked scent, so I replaced them with the fragrant 'Mary Rose'. Aside from this change, the herb garden has altered little from year to year. Maintaining it has fallen into a routine.

Every year I plant the left quadrants at the front and back with annual culinary herbs, such as basil, rosemary, and tarragon, behind the edge of assorted lavenders.

The right front bed is also edged with lavender but is planted with scented geraniums. Some are overwintered in the greenhouse and then are planted back out. Most start blooming in midspring indoors, which gives me the pleasure of their company both indoors and out, plus a chance to enjoy the beauty of their foliage and their fragrance over a long period. The variety of leaves—curled or crimped, fine or broad, velvety or rough, deep to light green, and even splashed or penciled with gold, silver, or cream—is extraordinary, and their scents are even more so, running the gamut from fruity to spicy to woody. I cut the foliage for flower arrangements and use bits as doilies under cheese or as garnish on food platters.

The right rear quadrant is a war zone between chives and whatever I plant next to them. Last year it was fennel. The year before, I tried basil. It was a race to see whether it would be the chives or the cold that would demolish the basil first. One of these days, I'll tire of the battle and let the chives have the space. No one told me chives should be confined and never let loose in a garden. Still, it is very useful in the kitchen, and when we have mild winters, I cut snips most of the year. Occasionally, chives jump clear out of the herb bed, but I catch the escapees and yank them out.

The mints follow the same pattern. After a few years, their aggressive behavior forced us to banish them to four pots situated around the circle. Overlooked ancestors persist, however, more than a decade later; every fragment of root that was missed sprouts and trespasses on its neighbors. But then, of course, we will always have enough to invite the neighborhood in for mint juleps.

Raising the herb bed made it clear to us that the drainage in the rest of the garden was poor. Still, a few years passed before we divided the main garden into 12 raised beds. Each one is 4 feet across, allowing us to reach the plants anywhere in the bed from outside it. We edged the beds with landscape ties stacked 2 feet high. This means the soil warms faster, we plant earlier, and our harvest is increased. In addition, the looser soil produces more perfectly shaped root crops. The ties are convenient to sit on while planting the beds, and there is no need to step on the soil and compress it.

We spread wood chips between the beds for easy walking and to suppress weeds. Over the following 20-plus years, as the aged chips broke down, we added new wood chips almost *(continued on page 38)*

In late June, the kitchen garden sees yellow chamomile finishing flowering, seeds sprouting, and leeks finally filling out. Mother Nature's nursery, where flowers self perpetuate, is at the back.

Vines draw the eye up, adding another

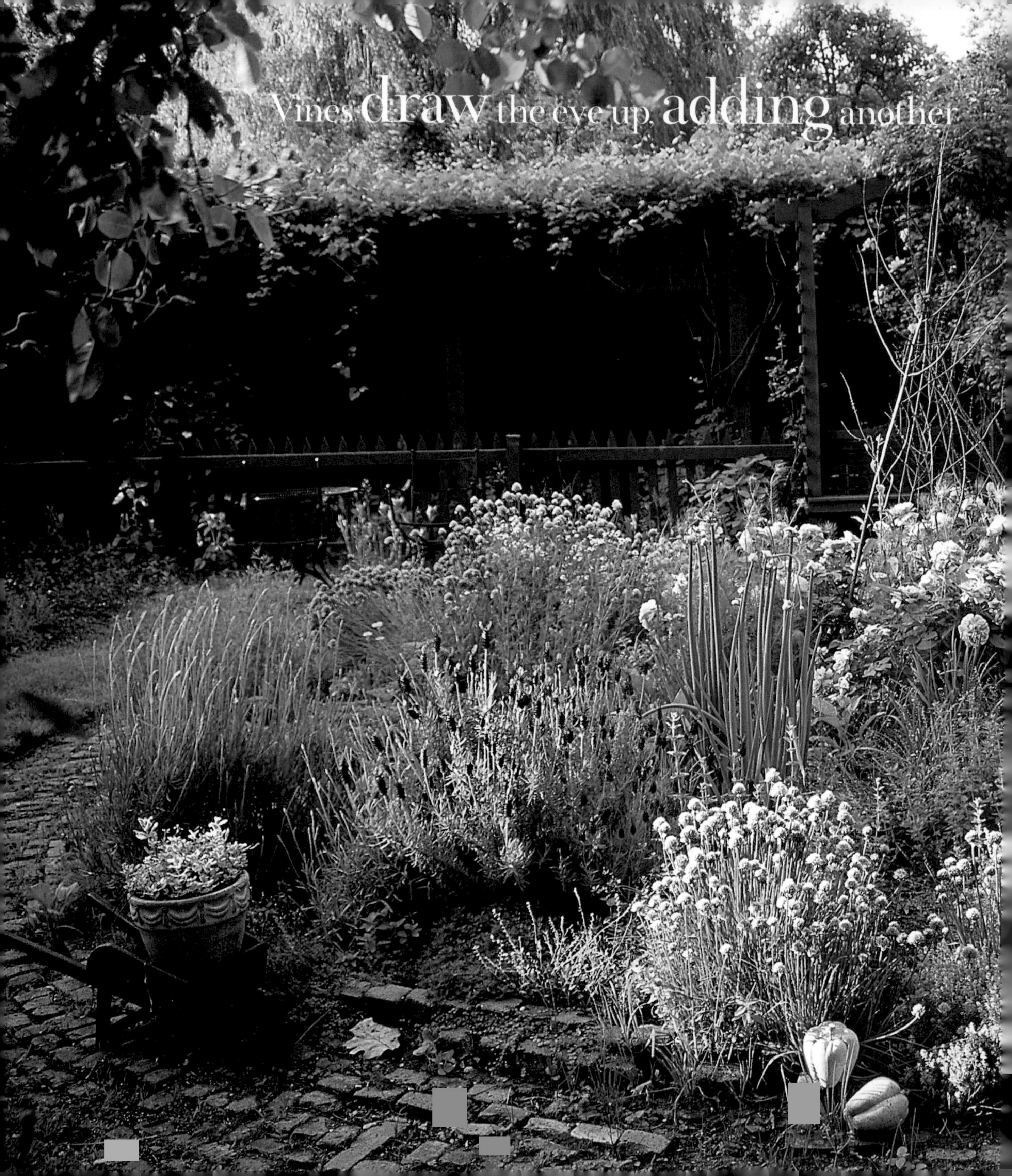

dimension to the garden.

The herb garden glows in
the early evening as the silver
foliage of lavender and
lamb's ears reflects the light.
The tepee of vitex branches in
the center of four roses
supports annual vines.

annually. I wasn't conscious of the slowly rising paths until they were almost as high as the raised beds. The process happened so gradually, it took an old picture to jog my memory. Under the wood chips, a rich topsoil gradually developed, inviting self-seeders to jump in and freely wander the paths. I move some, pull some, step on some, and ignore others. Frankly, I love the surprises.

Adding Structure

As the plants in the kitchen garden flourished, the chicken-wire fence surrounding it looked worse and worse. We replaced it with a white picket fence with two arbors, one arching over the gate and the other directly opposite with a built-in garden seat. It was there that I learned the importance of a garden seat. I am now convinced that no garden is complete without one. Seats encourage lingering, resting, and contemplating. We gardeners spend too little time in quiet admiration of our work.

We softened the starkness of the bright white fence by painting it park green, a dark, almost black green, and by cloaking it on three sides with a hedge of 'The Fairy' rose. The fourth side was already shaded by the crumbling remnants of a dilapidated grape arbor, complete with 80-year-old grapevines.

The new fence led us to look anew at the grape arbor, which we eventually rebuilt. Surprisingly, four of the seven original 80-year-old grapevines survived being moved four times in 2 years, and they still produce more grapes than we need. Their gnarled trunks add character to the arbor and support newly planted clematis. Because I couldn't restrain myself, the grape arbor is also draped with climbing roses, honeysuckle, wisteria, and clematis—a tapestry of color, texture, and fragrance.

Having painted the fence and realized how much difference color makes to the appearance of garden structures, I found that nothing has escaped my brush. The bench under the old oak became lichen green, matching the lichen on the tree's trunk. I painted the table and chairs by the water to match the blue of the bay and the sky on a sunny day, and I painted the bench alongside the lilac path lilac to chime with the flowers.

BELOW: The garden seat was originally planted with roses that clashed as they climbed: 'Aloha', 'Golden Showers', and 'Joseph's Coat'.
OPPOSITE: After a severe winter during which only 'Aloha' survived, we painted the seat park green and added another 'Aloha' to the other side. It was a great improvement.

We planted the new arbors with climbing roses; the one at the entrance got two 'Blaze' roses, one on each side. Incidentally, in my estimation, 'Blaze', even the new and improved one, tops the list of overrated, overmarketed roses. Gorgeous in late spring but distraught, depressed, and debilitated by the heat and humidity of summer, it fares only slightly better in fall. I replaced it after a few years with a vigorous 'New Dawn'—one of the best all-around-performing pink climbing roses. I now have no complaints. The 'New Dawn' arches at least 3 feet above the arbor and looks good enough to be cast in the movies.

We gardeners spend too little time in quiet admiration of our work.

In our hurry to get roses on the arbor around the garden seat, we planted all of our favorites: pink 'Aloha', yellow 'Golden Showers', red 'Don Juan' (my favorite for producing edible petals), and multicolored 'Joseph's Coat'. This blinding array of colors clashed as they climbed the arbor. Rather than change them, however, we named the garden seat the "electric chair" and made a point of enjoying the jolt of color and fragrance the roses delivered. In time three of the roses succumbed to an early death, victims of a combined severe winter and summer drought. Only 'Aloha' took everything in stride. We moved her twin to the other side of the arbor, but it will be a few years before she tops it.

No Straight Rows Here

Since we established the bones of the kitchen garden 25 years ago, they have not changed. The only straight lines are the fence and the wooden landscape ties. Around the perimeters of most beds, cascading plants such as nasturtiums hide the rough edges. It is an unpretentious and at times even untidy garden, unapologetically a jungle. All plants are welcome: perennials, annuals, roses, vines, herbs, vegetables, and bulbs. Flowers mingle freely with vegetables.

At first, I planted everything in rows. I covered the ground with black plastic and cut holes in it for the seeds and seedlings. Because the plastic looked unsightly, I covered it with salt hay. This was a tiresome chore. Plants rarely had a chance to self-seed. The joy of gardening was leaking away. A decade ago, I made a turnabout,

OPPOSITE: The whiskey barrel, painted green, is my "salad bowl," with lettuce and Johnny-jump-ups corralling chives.

The body of the "Little Woman" is made from a cylinder of green chicken wire cinched at the waist. She has garden gloves for hands and a beach ball for a head. Her dress is woven from annual climbing vines, such as climbing snapdragon (*Asarina scandens*), and nasturtiums.

planting seeds in groups rather than in straight lines. This way they enjoy the shade and support of each other's company while leaving no bare earth, as in a flower garden. No black plastic, no hoeing (although every few weeks there is some weeding). To refresh the soil, I plant winter rye in October in any empty space and use compost to fill up any hole where a plant has been removed or where soil in the bed is low. Planting sweet peas and beans with their nitrogen-fixing powers in a different bed each spring refreshes the soil naturally.

Some plants have constant spots in the garden—flowers and herbs, tomatoes (for the pleasure of picking and eating them right on the spot), zucchini (because its overproductivity feeds the neighbors as well as my ego), and potatoes (because they are better and more varied when homegrown)—but most move from bed to bed and gain different partners.

All of the raised beds change contents yearly, except the last one on the right, which is reserved for perennials and biennials that readily reseed—primarily foxgloves, sweet Williams, and lupines (see page 21). The whole of the front two beds and the ends of the beds bordering the main path are regularly planted with cutting flowers. This involves no special planning. When the seed catalogs arrive in January, I curl up in front of the fire and let my imagination run wild with possibilities. Practicality doesn't come into it. I overindulge, placing order after order. By the time the seeds arrive and it is time to plant, I wonder what I was

When the seed catalogs arrive, I curl up and let my imagination run wild with possibilities.

thinking. No matter. A few species are started indoors, but most are sown directly where they will flower. It is like Russian roulette—whatever seeds I have in my hand at the time go straight into the next bed. Color and height mean nothing here. The kitchen garden is a working garden—a garden to experiment in, a garden for play.

The only area I plant according to a plan is along the center path between the beds. When I look through the arbor, I want a frill of flowers on each side to lead my eye down the path. Like Monet, I love nasturtiums. By fall they will have sprawled beautifully over the wood chips. I toss the flowers in salads, use them for garnish, and include them in arrangements.

Cool-Weather Plantings

When the first warm days of spring arrive, I rush to work outside. All that pent-up energy needs to be put to good use. Cold-weather annuals and vegetables—peas, beans, potatoes, love-in-a-mist, alyssum, Shirley poppies (*Papaver rhoeas*), calendula, cleome, larkspur, sweet peas, snapdragons, sunflowers, and wishbone flower (*Torenia fournieri*)—are undaunted by flash freezing or dramatic swings in temperatures, so they can be sown first.

After sowing seeds, I throw garden blankets—helpers that deserve to be better known—on most of the seedbeds to speed germination. Garden blankets allow air, water, and 75 to 80 percent of the sun's rays to pass through while reducing evaporation and holding in heat. They also reduce soil erosion, prevent seeds from washing away, and protect new plants from flying insects, birds, and rabbits. They can stay without doing harm until the temperature nears 80°F, but they are usually long gone by then. The blankets come in twin-bed size, cost less than $10, and can be used over and over. I cut them, if necessary, to fit the bed. They take some getting used to: They look like white bedsheets blown off the clothesline onto the garden. Because early spring is too soon for most garden visitors, however, they remain my little secret.

As an example of what a garden blanket can do, consider this: One year I planted nasturtiums in one corner of the garden, but by the time they had sprouted, I decided I wanted more in another part of the garden. So I planted another batch and covered it with a blanket. Within a month, the second group had surpassed the first planting.

Garden blankets look like sheets blown off the line onto the beds, but they greatly speed up germination and growth.

Pieces of blanket can also be used later to protect plants from too much sun. This might well be the case if you are transplanting annuals in the heat of the day. Prop the blanket up horizontally, tied between a triangle of three bamboo poles, as a canopy to shade the plants for a few days without trapping heat.

I plant the kitchen garden mostly from seed each spring, generally ignoring the information given on the seed packet. Seed companies tend to play it safe, recommending that almost everything be planted after the danger of frost has past. This spoils the fun, restricting the garden season to the months of the year without frost. Why should I wait until late May when experience has taught me that many seeds can be sown as soon as the soil can be worked, in late March or early April? At first I thought it was a gamble. Then I realized many of the seeds I was sowing were self-seeding from the year before and surviving perfectly well (though not necessarily where I wanted them). So I added them to my list of early sowers.

SWEET PEAS AND SHIRLEY POPPIES

Sweet peas (*Lathyrus odoratus*), I read in an antique garden book, could be sowed outdoors in December in Pennsylvania. Intuitively, they know to sprout in late winter when the weather allows. So I gave it a try. During the first week of December, I dug a narrow trench 1½ feet deep around the green wooden obelisk where sweet peas were to grow. I filled it with a mix of compost, well-rotted manure, a sprinkling of lime, and the soil I'd removed in equal parts to within 6 inches of ground level. (Sweet peas demand rich food and long cool drinks.) I poked the seeds 2 inches deep and 3 to 4 inches apart in the trench, watered them in, and left them alone until warm days arrived. The trench collected and held water while the sunken seedbed protected the seedlings from damaging winds and severe cold. As the seedlings sprouted, I hoed in soil to hold them upright and to force the roots to run deeper, thus keeping them cool. Once the seedlings reached ground level, I added a few more inches of compost around their base. Blooms started after 3 months of strong growth.

I have since followed this pattern with great success. During the period of strong growth, temperatures of 50° to 60°F are ideal. As long as the roots stay cool and moist and the flowers are removed before they go

Sweet peas planted outside in December on Long Island are climbing almost to the top of the obelisk by June.

to seed, the plants bloom. Some years, when the nights stay cool, the sweet peas flower for 3 months or longer. A prolonged heat spell slows their production. And if I stop cutting the flowers—even a week can make a difference—the plants go to seed with lightning speed and flower production ceases.

To hedge my bets, I always start a few packs of sweet peas indoors under grow lights in February. If I start them later, I keep the grow lights on around the clock and check twice daily to see if they need water. (It is another garden myth that seeds need both day and night to grow.) However, the seeds sown directly outdoors usually produce stronger plants.

The fragile and delicate **Shirley poppies** (*Papaver rhoeas*) keep coming for many weeks if a cluster is sown every week or two for successive weeks starting in March. They disappear rather quickly once hot weather settles in. Though they have a short vase life, all stages of their development are attractive—from the demurely nodding bud to the flower dancing on its wiry stem and, finally, the ornamental seed capsule.

THE SALAD BOWL

In early spring I plant a mosaic of lettuce and salad greens in one bed of the kitchen garden and supplement this with a green half whiskey barrel—my "salad

A mosaic of assorted lettuces and red cabbage is as colorful as flowers.

bowl"—edged with lettuce and holding cherry tomatoes that dangle down the sides. The half-barrel adds height and whimsy next to the low-growing lettuce bed. As the lettuce in the bed finishes, the space is up for grabs. I might plant it with flowers or kale or something I've never grown before.

POTATOES

Potatoes have been my favorite food for as long as I can remember. (That's no secret to my friends, who sent me an arrangement of potatoes and flowers for my birthday.) Yet until a decade ago it had never occurred to me to grow them. After tasting some grown by Rosalind Creasy, the author of *Cooking from the Garden,* I have discovered they are oh-so-much better straight from the ground. Many specialty potatoes are so flavorful they don't need butter. 'Yellow Finn' and 'German Butterball', with their rich yellow coloring, taste and look as if they are already buttered.

'All Blue' is the best of the blue potatoes, although I find the lavender-colored flesh off-putting. I only grew them once; it was a passing fancy. If they grew fast enough to be harvested for a red, white, and blue potato salad on the Fourth of July, I might plant them again, but for no other reason. Other potatoes are tastier.

Potatoes are early risers and can be planted as soon as the soil can be worked in spring. Often that's March, although I usually don't get around to it until mid-April. They shouldn't be planted where their cousins—peppers, tomatoes, and eggplant— have grown in the previous 2 years. They are susceptible to the same diseases and pass them back and forth in the soil.

Potatoes develop from swellings of their roots and can be harvested at any size—and consequently at any time. I often "rob" the hills in the middle of summer for a special treat of little new potatoes, which can be done without damaging the plant or the rest of the crop if you are careful.

OTHER VEGETABLES

Because it is a place to experiment, where anything goes, the kitchen garden has more stories to tell than any of the other gardens. This is the place I try new plants and repeat old favorites. The Chinese tag the years with the names of animals—the year of the

An assortment of tomatoes in all sizes and shapes grow in the kitchen garden, including currant tomatoes, cherry tomatoes, yellow tomatoes, and plum tomatoes.

monkey, the year of the dragon, and so forth; I remember mine by the weird or wonderful vegetables and flowers we grew.

There was the summer of the Chinese vegetables, when the cucuzzi squash, tucked in among the more conventional snow peas, pak choi, and Chinese cabbage, took off with the speed of a race car skidding on ice. It leaped over the fence into the rose hedge and ran out across the lawn 20 feet or more to the brick walk. All along the vine were giant torpedo- or S-shaped cucumber-like fruits, some as long as 4 feet and as wide as 5 inches. As soon as I spied the kids fencing with the largest of these, I knew the plant had captured their attention. It was good for little else, alas—soup made with it was so tasteless that I never cooked it again. But I grew the cucuzzi for years simply to enjoy the miracle of its quick growth. One year I forgot to save the seeds, and I've never found it for sale again.

The summer of the tomato medley was tame by comparison. Until then I had grown only red tomatoes, never yellow, pink, or green ones. Favorites from that summer are with me still—'Brandywine', 'Yellow Pear', and the currant tomato, a different species entirely. The name, currant tomato, describes their fruit size. They can be plucked and popped into your mouth on the spot. They line the ends of the stems like cherry tomatoes, each ripening in succession, so they are a

One of the strangest vegetables we grew is the cucuzzi squash. The vine sprinted 20 feet across the lawn and each squash measured a yard or more.

A garden of this sort encourages experimentation because it need not be beautiful, only productive.

colorful mix of red and green and all shades in between. Their tiny size makes them a topic of conversation on a salad or as a garnish.

Then there was the Mexican summer of peppers, tomatillos, and cilantro—probably best forgotten. The summer was too cool for the peppers, natives of tropical and semitropical regions. The tomatillos will be with me forever as they self-seed incorrigibly. I try to let only one plant mature, providing a branch

or two for flower arrangements. The light green, golf-ball–size fruit is covered with a paper husk that I find decorative. Although their flavor has been likened to that of green apples, I have yet to find a recipe using them that I would repeat.

ANNUAL FLOWERING VINES

It was from photographs of the kitchen garden that I first grasped the value of flowering vines and their softening touch. They do more to enhance a garden than almost anything else. Vines draw the eye up, adding another dimension to the garden. As I became more interested in vines, I replaced our simple tepee structures and trellises with taller metal columns, plus a decorative birdhouse on a 10-foot pole. The birdhouse on the pole looked good, but it wasn't practical for climbers. Few vines shimmy up a pole by themselves. The birdhouse migrated to the center of a cluster of hydrangeas along the woodland walk. We finally settled on two wooden obelisks, each giving us four sides for vines to climb on. To give the vines a leg up, we wrapped the bottom half of the obelisks in black bird netting. The fine netting is almost invisible, yet it is strong enough for a vine to grip and pull itself up on.

Twelve years ago, at the entrance to the path between the beds, we built a temporary arbor made of an iron reinforcing rod threaded through sections of old garden hose and bent into an arch. The end of each rod plunged a foot deep into the ground for balance. Vitex branches tied to the arch helped the vines climb. The structure turned out to be stable and surprised us by standing there sturdily for 2 years. Realizing that it looked lonely and out of scale with the path, we added two more. A few years later, all these gave way to a permanent wooden arbor in keeping with the one over the gate and the other over the garden seat, but twice as wide.

The race of annual vines over the arbor is always a pleasure to watch. I don't place bets, though—I know who will win. **Love-in-a-puff** (*Cardiospermum halicacabum*) always leads off, with sweet peas close behind. The sweet peas stop below the 5-foot mark, just as summer heats up. Then the heat nudges the morning glories, and they sprint ahead. My favorite, the wacky, silver-leafed **woolly morning glory** (*Argyreia nervosa*), is right out of *Little Shop of Horrors*. An *Ipomoea* cousin with sinuous, strong limbs that climb 15 to 20 feet in summer, its heart-shaped leaves are 10 inches wide with downy white undersides with a silver sheen. In the long, hot summers of its native India, it grows 30 to 40 feet, putting out 3- to 4-foot tendrils.

OPPOSITE, LEFT, AND ABOVE, LEFT: Both crimson starglory (*Ipomoea lobata*) and the cup-and-saucer vine (*Cobaea scandens*) are tall annual vines that wait until fall to flower. OPPOSITE, RIGHT, AND ABOVE, RIGHT: Morning glories shimmy up a 10-foot pole to garland a birdhouse and climb iron reinforcing bars to make an apparent living arbor.

Clipped chaste tree (*Vitex agnus-castus*) branches make a strong bean trellis.

These have grabbed me many times as I walk by. I weave it through the wooden slats, where it belongs, until it frees itself again. I haven't yet seen it flower, but no matter: The silvery limbs and leaves are decorative enough. When it does flower, I'm told, its morning-glory–like flowers are lavender with a downy coat. So far, I've grown it only as an annual, but last fall I cut it back to a foot before a heavy frost, dug it up, and put it in a pot in the laundry room for a winter of dormancy. The laundry room has moist air and two eyebrow windows, so it gets a little light as well as moisture. Every month or two I give it a bit of water. In May I'll return it to the garden; then perhaps it'll bloom.

Climbing snapdragons, nasturtiums, and the other gentle climbers haven't much of a chance to reach the heights of the arbor. They bloom densely over the bottom 4 feet. The **cup-and-saucer vine** (*Cobaea scandens*) and **crimson starglory** (*Ipomoea lobata*) move more slowly than the morning glories, but by fall they pass the other vines. Their late blooming in fall and long after the first frost assures that all eyes are on them.

Hyacinth bean (*Dolichos lablab*) is usually given its own tower; it likes to take over, climbing 10 to 30 feet in summer. Contrary to its common name, it is neither a hyacinth nor a bean. Its plentiful purple flowers bloom on long spikes and remind me more of sweet peas than hyacinths. They can be cut and plopped in a vase for a colorful arrangement. The flat, seed-filled, velvety purple pods are even more decorative. For a pick-me-up-and-knock-me-out fall centerpiece, bunch the purple pods with orange and red dahlias, blue salvias, and red fall foliage in a carved-out pumpkin shell.

Moonflower (*Ipomoea alba*) is temperamental and doesn't always germinate. If I start it indoors, it sometimes falters when moved outside. I plant it every year; some years it succeeds, and others it doesn't. I am charmed by its fragrance and romanced by the way it lights up the night. I get a kick out of grabbing an early drink, say at five o'clock, and watching its salad-plate–size flowers open in jerky starts.

I have a particular affection for **scarlet runner beans** (*Phaseolus coccineus*). They traveled to America with the Pilgrims, who valued them for their foot-long pods of edible beans. I am more enamored of their clusters of brilliant scarlet, pealike flowers. Scarlet is always eye-catching. Still, everything about this vine—the heart-shaped leaves, the shapely beans, the bright scarlet seeds and flowers—is attractive. The seeds can be sown directly into the garden after all danger of frost is past and will quickly grow 15 feet or more, with nonstop flowering and bean production despite heavy frost. They also improve the soil's fertility. After they die back in fall,

Planting sweet peas and beans with their nitrogen-fixing powers in a different bed each spring refreshes the soil naturally.

I turn the stalks into the soil. Scarlet runner beans share the pea family trait of fixing nitrogen in the soil, thus making it available to other plants the next year.

Every spring we make a fence of **chaste tree** (*Vitex agnus-castus*) branches as a bean trellis. When I cut the shrubs back in the formal garden each January, I save the branches, which are strong and flexible, perfect for staking perennials. To make a bean trellis out of them, push Y-shaped branches into the ground in a series of overlapping Ys, tying them together with twine where they touch. Simple and practical. (See beans growing on the vitex fence on the opposite page.)

SUNFLOWERS

The vegetable garden wouldn't be complete without an assortment of sunflowers, especially the giant ones, grown for their smiley disposition. I defy you to look any sunflower in the eye and refrain from smiling. When these incredibly optimistic flowers flaunt their personalities, it's almost impossible to be glum. Perhaps they bring out the child in us.

I value mammoth sunflowers almost as much in winter. I always leave a few to dry and feed the birds. The strongest ones stand tall clear through winter. Capped by snow, their drooping heads almost look human.

Growing sunflowers requires a certain sense of humor. Years ago, I planted a flowering shrub border

a garden vignette

When my children were young, we would tie a yellow ribbon around the neck of a sunflower, just when it was the height of our smallest child. The sunflower shot up so fast that the ribbon was out of reach within a week or two; the kids had to crick their necks to see the blossom. Fascination grew along with the plant. By summer's end, they were climbing on each other's shoulders to reach it.

along the entrance of our driveway for privacy, but the shrubs were small and needed a few years to mature. So I lined up a dozen 'Mammoth' sunflowers as a decorative screen. 'Mammoth' stands 10 to 12 feet tall with the heads a foot or more across. Surely a regiment of sunflowers is as imposing as a regiment of guards at Buckingham Palace. But everyone who passed by snickered. Sunflowers have that effect. Of course, when the shrubs matured and I no longer needed the sunflowers, people missed them and complained!

I defy you to look any sunflower in the eye and refrain from smiling.

The kitchen garden offers me real—and welcome—latitude. Because my plant selections are often based on emotion, the choices may make sense only to me. Not everything has to be beautiful. Some are quirky, some are wacky, some are downright silly, but they are all mine. I grow love-in-a-puff for its black seeds with white hearts, moonflower for its heavenly fragrance, love-in-a-mist for its wanton ways, tomatoes for the pleasure of picking and eating in the garden, giant sunflowers for their personality, and climbing roses for something to look up to. The red cockscomb celosia I planted to dry for Christmas wreaths turned out to be even more bizarre than I expected. One plant held its red flowers up, forming a fist with one finger extended. Garden photographers came from miles around for pictures that enlivened many a garden lecture. Of course, growing hardy gladiolas has ruined my reputation for good taste.

Now that we know more about gardening, we have time to be playful. What could be better examples of this than our scarecrows? We have always had at least one. One year we got carried away and made two: "The Little Woman," with chicken-wire bones and a dress of nasturtiums and climbing snapdragons topped by a lacy alyssum collar (see page 42); and her counterpoint, "Pot Man," a figure made with stacks of different-size pots. Some people might regard this as hopelessly unsophisticated, but I've always felt that if visitors find things to smile at in the garden, they're more likely to enjoy it. And a garden, after all, is to be enjoyed.

OPPOSITE: A wreath of assorted fall leaves (peony, oak, and maple) and berries punctuated with a sunflower seedhead feeds the birds and decorates the garden gate.

The Woodland Walk

Our first extensive planting was in the shade of the woodland. I was more familiar then with woodland plants and flowers than with sun-drenched gardens, so I started with what I knew. In my 20s, I had lived and gardened in the

In spring, before the trees leaf out, the woodland walk is awash in blooms, including red species tulips, Virginia bluebells, grape hyacinths, Mayapples, and assorted yellow and white daffodils.

woods of upstate New York. Short on money and long on dreams, I created my first gardens by transplanting native woodland flowers from our own woods into beds near the house.

I now sought out the ones I fondly remembered—trillium, lobelia, columbine, wood geranium, Welsh poppies, Jack-in-the-pulpit—in catalogs and nurseries for our new garden.

t he existing woodland walk was a dirt fire lane some 120 yards long, cut into the hillside so in an emergency a fire truck could reach the bay for water. The woods themselves, a little more than an acre lying to the north and east of the house, gently sloped to the bay. Over the course of several years, starting at the top of the walk and working my way down, I planted both sides with bulbs, perennials, groundcovers, shrubs, and wildflowers. I knew enough to plant bulbs in clumps and the perennials in groups of five or seven, but there was no overall plan. Combinations were hit or miss.

Eventually, at the bottom of the path where it wraps around the back of the house, we added two ponds. The smallest is nestled into the hillside off the kitchen terrace. It flows into a stream, rushes downhill, and leaps over a waterfall before splashing into the larger pond filled with goldfish, water lilies, and lotus. A hidden pump returns the water to the top. At the large pond, where the woodland walk ends, a flat, shady patch widens out into a small stone terrace. It is a pleasant, cool place to sit or to eat a meal on a hot day.

I realized a few years ago that the woodland walk needed more ornamental trees and shrubs to connect the bulbs at ground level with the blooms in the high canopy of the tulip trees. The yellow blossoms of the tulip trees—both flowers and leaves resemble tulips—are difficult to see, but Mother Nature apparently doesn't want them to be missed and drops bunches of them to the ground. They land in all their perfection and cover the path for several weeks. Sometimes I collect them to float in a glass bowl. A good many do not fall but cling to the branches, ripen, and dry, perching decoratively upright through the following winter.

In a perfect world a garden designer would start by placing the trees, then the shrubs, and finally the perennials, annuals, and groundcovers. I did it upside down. In the early years, my husband planted azaleas, forsythia, and rhododendron to hide the fence between the properties. The junipers found their own way in. A few shrubs—nandina, kerria, assorted hydrangeas, and tree peonies—were added in spurts, but not enough of them. Nearly 20 years passed before I finally got around to adding half a dozen ornamental trees and a dozen flowering shrubs to provide a bridge between the earthbound plants and the tops of the trees. I know now that a variety of plants growing at different heights causes the eye to move up and down, adding depth, interest, and beauty to the woods.

The larger pond at the bottom of the hill is filled with perennial water lilies, lotus, and fish. Hydrangeas bloom around the edge.

t

Spring Awakening

he woodland walk grows more beautiful each year. There are many reasons for this, but surely one of the most important is the spring bulbs. They kick-start the gardening year and provide any garden's most glorious moments. The easiest path from rags to riches is to plant more bulbs.

Over the last 20 years, Siberian squill has naturalized on the hillside so that early daffodils bloom in a sea of blue.

Spring Bulbs

besides their vigor and willingness to multiply, spring bulbs are marvels at coping with whatever the climate sends their way. Known for their sheer cockiness and unflagging courage, they have perfected survival techniques. When the temperatures rise above freezing, the bulbs rush to bloom, bringing the garden its first flush of color. Hit by snow, sleet, and ice, they simply close up, patiently waiting for the weather to change, and then open up again. I've seen many bulbs lie down and play dead on a snowy, windy, or rainy day only to rise again as soon as the sun shines. I wonder how they do it.

Both windflowers and crocuses close tightly each night, keeping the frost at bay, thus extending their bloom for several weeks. Snowdrops, glory-of-the-snow, and dwarf irises simply stop growing in a deep freeze, waiting for a pleasant turn in the weather before they shoot up another inch or two. I can't resist cutting a handful of snowdrops to bring indoors. Plunked in water, the bottom ½ inch of their hollow stems coil up tightly like four snippets of curling ribbon. In a glass vase, it makes a pretty picture.

Blue puschkinia (*Puschkinia scilloides*), another hardy soul, has a singular habit of blooming the moment its bud pushes through the ground. If the weather is not to its liking, it lays its head on the ground and waits for better times before stretching up to its full 6 inches and sprouting foliage. The nodding bells are the faded blue of worn denim, with delicate white pinstripes visible only up close.

Spring starflower (*Ipheion uniflorum*) takes its weather watching to an extreme. These lazy fellows refuse to open if the day is dreary. I sympathize. They pull the covers over their heads and take a nap, saving themselves for fair weather. This may be why they bloom for such a long time—often 6 weeks or more. They don't send up all of their blue starry flowers at once. The flowers have a sweet mint scent. However, the floppy, grasslike foliage, if bruised or broken, smells like peeled onions.

Species tulips—*tarda* is a good example—open out wide during the day and close at night. Many stay in bloom longer than the hybrids. Hybrid tulips, on the other hand, are more fragile. The parrot tulips especially need to be placed in a protected spot or picked shortly after they bloom and brought inside. That's why I grow them in the kitchen garden.

The **crown imperial** (*Fritillaria imperialis*) is a handsome, stately flower. Atop its strong 3- to 4-foot stem is a circle of large yellow, red, or burnt orange nodding bells, topped with a tufted crown of green leaves. If you peer inside each bell, you'll witness the most peculiar sight: clear drops of nectar, or "heaven's collected tears," as Shelley poetically put it. They glisten, are smooth to the touch, and are sweet on the tongue. Produced in a tiny cavity at the base of each bell, the nectar is vital for the flower to set seed and is replaced if removed—again and again, if necessary.

Crown imperial (*Fritillaria imperialis*) holds court over mid- to late-blooming daffodils.

The fact that the crown imperial **bulb** and its flowers smell like rotting meat doesn't deter me from planting it or picking a few blossoms for the house. Flowers with good looks can get away with body odor. I mask the scent with powerfully fragrant daffodils or hyacinths.

Some gardeners have dubbed *Fritillaria* "the problem child of the lily family." It isn't that it is difficult. It simply expects its perfectly reasonable requests to be granted, and we're not always sure what those requests are. The genus is a curious and strange group with mostly nodding or droopy flowers in purples, chocolate, white, and yellow. The McClure & Zimmerman catalog has 18 different listings. I'm slowly working my way through them. So far the only one I can count on to return is the snake's head fritillary, but it is good to continue challenging myself by throwing a few jokers into the pack. A couple might surprise me.

Daffodils and **wood hyacinths** are just the opposite of fritillaries. They are extremely dependable bulbs. I layer them under the taller, tougher groundcovers—pachysandra, myrtle, and St. John's-wort. The groundcover blankets the bulbs, protecting them from freezing and thawing in a temperamental winter. During heavy spring rains, mud won't splatter and spoil their appearance. If the groundcover blooms at the same time as the **bulbs**—say myrtle and early daffs—they just put on a better show.

day only to rise again as soon as the sun shines.

I could almost be content planting only daffodils, an old reliable. The family dresses up in so many different costumes and comes at such different times over the course of 2 to 3 months, depending on how long and drawn-out spring weather is. I don't plant the common trumpeters—'King Alfred' is the best known—preferring unique and distinct characters. 'February Gold' is always the first to bloom and is quick to naturalize. Among the petite April-flowering daffodils, I like 'Tête-à-Tête' and 'Thalia' for their multiple flowers on each stem. 'Tête-à-Tête' has several shades of yellow while 'Thalia', also known as the

The easiest path from rags to riches is to plant more bulbs.

'Orchid Narcissus', is white. 'Jenny', a dainty little daffodil 10 inches high, flaunts her good looks by flipping her white petals back. 'Peeping Tom', a deep yellow with a long narrow trumpet, looks like a nosy nerd. Among the late-blooming doubles, 'Cheerfulness', 'Erlicheer', and 'White Lion' are among the most beautiful and powerfully perfumed. 'Pheasant's Eye' and 'Actaea' are among the last to bloom, and they carry a fragrance that intrigues me.

Each fall I can't resist planting a few dozen tulips. The perennial collection from White Flower Farm has been faithfully returning for 10 years even though I didn't follow their advice about planting: Instead of planting in full sun as recommended, I planted the tulips at the edge of the woods in a shady border. They have done fine. This perennial collection consists of Darwin hybrids in single colors. I'm now putting together my own clumps from among the Darwin hybrids offered. Two other tulips that returned for more than 5 years are 'Queen of the Night', a dark purple, almost black tulip, and 'Orange Parrot', which has feathery petals in shrieking orange and a heavy perfume.

PLANTING BULBS

Planting depth is not an exact science, although many bulb charts imply otherwise. Most charts recommend planting daffodils, for example, with their bottoms 8 inches below the surface. They don't take into account that daffodil bulbs come in different sizes, some miniatures being smaller than snowdrop or crocus bulbs. Nor do the charts take into account the type of soil. Generally, bulbs should be planted deeper in sandy soil than in clay. Even the old rule of thumb—plant a bulb three times deeper than its size—works for only some, not all. For example, crinum lilies are larger then daffs but sit just below the surface.

So depth doesn't worry me much. Most bulbs have the ability to move up and down. Some smaller ones will even flip over if planted upside down. In the wild, of course, a daffodil or snowdrop drops its seed on top of the ground. The seed somehow works its way down into the soil as it stores up food, growing for several years before blooming.

In a garden, the shortest plants traditionally go in front and the taller ones in the back, but in early spring, such niceties don't matter. The garden is largely bare. Most perennials don't make an appearance until late April or May, and the early arrivals—lungwort, sweet woodruff, barrenwort, *Epimedium,* and primroses— are generally shorter. Many of the evergreen groundcovers, such as bunchberry, creeping variegated euonymus, pachysandra, and vinca, hug the ground. So the earliest bulb bloomers—from snowdrops to miniature daffodils—can be scattered about the garden without much regard for height. Height is only an issue when planting bulbs into a groundcover or next to a taller early perennial such as hellebores. Then I choose varieties that are tall enough to peek over the foliage.

To plant a large number of bulbs at one time and to extend the bloom in the same spot, I often dig a bucket-size hole, 8 inches deep and 14 inches wide,

a garden vignette

A plant combination I favor is the snake's head fritillary, the crown imperial's cousin, blooming atop the polished petite oval leaves of winter creeper (*Euonymus fortunei* 'Gracilis'). Snake's head fritillary is a unique character with many common names—guinea-hen and checkered lily are two. (The more common names a flower has indicates how much it is loved.) Superbly mottled with a fascinating checkered design in muted shades of bronze, purple, and white, it should be copied on silk and made into a blouse. I've got the perfect suit to wear with it.

and layer it with 25 to 40 bulbs depending on their size and favored depth. In the bottom, I might place six late-blooming daffodils circling a crown imperial, cover them, and then place a dozen Siberian squill 4 inches from the top. After they are tucked in, I'll squeeze in another dozen snowdrops 2 inches from the top. The bloom time of the snowdrops and squill might overlap, but both will be gone before the daffodils open. When the crown imperial blooms in the midst of the late daffodils, it is a curious sight. I imagine the crown imperial is holding court, looking down his droopy blooms at the daffodils, while the daffs are trumpeting up at him. One clump is never enough. I repeat the layered planting with a minimum of three bucket-size holes nearby, and the bulbs put on a nice show.

Narcissus 'Baby Moon'

Narcissus 'Minnow'

Narcissus 'Bridal Crown'

Narcissus 'Little Gem'

Narcissus 'Tete-a-Tete'

Narcissus 'White Lion'

Narcissus bulbocodium var. conspicuus

Narcissus 'Hawath'

Early spring bulbs may be small and meek, but

Another approach to planting bulbs is to dig a trench and fill it with two layers—say wood hyacinth on the bottom and glory-of-the-snow on top. The glory-of-the-snow blooms and disappears before the wood hyacinth comes up. Or the smallest bulbs can be poked in under the foliage of an existing spreading groundcover—lungwort, ginger, ivy, creeping euonymus, or a patch of lawn—without preparing the soil at all. But then I do spread compost on a yearly basis.

When planting tulips, crocus, or other tasty bulbs, I cover them with a piece of chicken wire, anchored with 6-inch-long hairpin-shaped pieces of wire to keep the squirrels and other pests from digging them up and eating them. Some books recommend planting the bulbs in wire cages, which is a lot of trouble. Chicken wire is easier and can be covered with compost. The stems have no trouble finding their way up and through the chicken wire. Our squirrels are too lazy to dig in sideways. In any case, they have acorns and walnuts and other earthy delights nearby, just waiting to be picked up. Squirrels are more apt to unearth newly planted bulbs, when the digging is easy, than established ones; after the first spring, they rarely bother. Thank God, they don't touch the daffodils, colchicums, scillas, and other poisonous bulbs.

MOVING BULBS

Bulbs are easily dug up, divided, moved, and replanted. If I don't like their placement, if the colors clash, or if I see a bare spot and want to steal a few bulbs from an established planting to start a new colony, I just do it. I've moved bulbs in bloom with no ill effect. It is the fresh look that comes from shuffling plants, like rearranging the furniture inside the house, that makes gardening an exciting art.

The solution to a lackluster planting may be as simple as moving daffodils from one side of the driveway to the other in order to hitch them to a forsythia, kerria, or flowering quince. A smarter approach is to make spring lists of existing plants needing partners and new couples to invite to the party. (As an added incentive, many bulb catalogs reward orders placed before the end of June with a discounted price and don't charge until the bulbs are shipped.) For ideas about what goes with what, I look around the yard, down the block, and all over town to see what's blooming simultaneously.

OPPOSITE: Daffodils come in all different sizes. The largest are planted 8 inches deep while the smallest can be planted 4 or 5 inches deep.

their ability to **roll** with the punches is miraculous.

You can divide daffodils in spring when their heads are above ground. I have even been successful in moving them while they are in bloom if I use a pitchfork, dig deeply, lift, gently pull the bulbs apart, and immediately replant.

When it comes to bulbs, bigger is not always better. Less is more. The lower the price, the higher the probability they will naturalize. Early spring bulbs may be small and meek, but their ability to roll with the punches, then go forth and multiply is miraculous. Many are among nature's most care-free plants, undemanding and adaptable. It took me a while to learn this, and I didn't discover it from browsing through glossy bulb catalogs; instead, I observed the shady bank around the ponds. Originally, this bank was planted with a few patches of Siberian squill, glory-of-the-snow, snowdrops, and a lot of grass. Not wanting to mow a hillside, I dug up the grass and weeds and introduced shade-loving groundcovers to civilize the area. It never occurred to me as I was amending the soil—digging holes and adding compost—that the small bulbs would survive the new regime, let alone flourish.

Yet that is exactly what happened. On the hillside, they are utterly free to roam, and they make use of their freedom. I already knew that they multiply both by dropping seed and by producing tiny bulblets around the base of the mother bulb— the largest might be about the size of a marble. (I sometimes find groups of tiny bulbs lying on top of the ground in fall; I poke them in to help them along.) What I didn't realize was that the law of compound interest works here. As the numbers of bulbs grew, the rate of increase accelerated until the blue of the hillside squill matched that of the sky. Good reason to plant plenty to begin with. Why wait? A few hundred bulbs cost less than a bouquet of flowers. With proper planting, they'll bloom faithfully for decades.

Now the hillside has scatter rugs of snowdrops in midwinter and a blue wall-to-wall carpet of Siberian squill in late winter. It has become a cavalry of advancing bulbs. I'm convinced that most of the spring bulbs I've planted, or their babies, will be here long after I've gone.

Spring Woodland Perennials

When the bulbs are successfully partnered with early-blooming perennials, the woodland awakens, sirens blaring in bold crayon colors. Many early perennials' buds emerge from the ground fully formed, mimicking bulbs. Hellebores are one of them, and one of the few perennials visible year-round.

HELLEBORES

Hellebores (*Helleborus*) are in constant flower in spring and are among the first to bloom and the last to leave. From midwinter until late spring, bulbs like snowdrops, winter aconite, and crocus come and go, but hellebores are still carrying on when the wood hyacinth and columbines waltz in. Then they quietly step back to provide a lush green background for summer flowers.

When winter is at its most dismal, dark, and dank, we are blessed with their drooping, buttercup-shaped flowers. The contrast is a happy one, enriched yet more by the knowledge that this miracle of flowers blooming in the snow is the promise of so many more to follow. I'm a great admirer of hellebores' quiet determination, good looks, and easygoing manner. They are as close to perfection as nature ever created. Still, timing is everything; if they bloomed in summer, I might pay them very little heed.

Hellebore colors range from the bride white of *H. niger* to the lime green of *H. foetidus* and the muted pinks, mauves, and purples of *H. orientalis* and *H. × hybridus.* It is actually the sepals rather than the petals that carry the color. The petals are inconspicuous nectaries. Over the months of bloom, the sepals—whatever their original color—fade to a lime green. This suits me fine because that green provides a wonderful contrast to brighter colors in flower arrangements.

In our woodland, hellebores flourish in heavy clay under the shade of deciduous trees where other perennials gave up after only a year or two. *H. niger,* commonly called the Christmas rose, is the first to bloom, displaying clusters of bright snowy white sepals. The cup-shaped flowers, sometimes speckled with purple, open out flat like saucers, up to 2½ inches across, to show off their yellow stamens. (Legend has it that this thornless "rose" suddenly opened at the very hour when Jesus was born. That may be, but a hellebore is not even remotely related to a rose.) The deep green foliage is compound, divided into seven or more leaflets, with serrated edges that can scratch the unwary. New foliage replaces the old quickly at winter's end.

H. foetidus has at least two common names—bear's foot hellebore and stinking hellebore. I don't find an odor unless I put my nose in the flower, close my eyes to concentrate, and breathe deeply. Indoors, the flowers are odorless. The tight-lipped, lime green clusters of bells gleam along the edge with a smudge of maroon lipstick that becomes more pronounced as they age. Unlike *H. orientalis* and *H. niger,* whose flowering stems are bare of foliage, *H. foetidus* has leaf sprays springing from its flow-

Lenten roses (*Helleborus orientalis*) hybridize freely among themselves, yielding flowers in many shades of pink.

ering stem. The flowering stem is already a foot high when winter begins and the buds are formed, protected by light green foliage. How the buds survive snow and frost, I don't know, but they do.

Lenten rose (*H. orientalis*) blooms next with pink- or purple-tinged flowers. Although most hellebores are native to England, even the English admit the labeling of hellebores is confusing. Many of the hellebores sold as *H. orientalis* are in fact hybrids and should be named *H. × hybridus.* In my own garden I originally planted these three species, and a decade later, after many marriages among the three, I have gathered and moved hundreds of hybrid seedlings from under the skirts of their mothers to new parts of the garden. Some garden books proclaim that hellebores like lime, and maybe they do, yet they thrive in my acid garden. I never add lime, but I do spread compost or shredded leaves around them yearly.

I yearn for the hellebores I see pictured in English and Irish gardens—yellow, black-purple, and rosy clear pink with petals in double ruffles. No doubt in the near future they will cross the ocean and I, too, can grow them. Anticipation is one of the many pleasures of gardening.

Most years hellebores and snowdrops bloom in February; occasionally, it's January. According to my journal, it has been March in 2 of the last 15 years. I notice that the entry in my garden journal on February 27, 1991, reads, "The hellebore flowers are a foot high, open and perfect, completely undamaged by the winter

Plants growing at different heights cause the eye to move up and down, adding depth, interest, and beauty.

weather, although their foliage is ragged and about to collapse." The entry of March 7, 1993, reads, "After an unusually cold and destructive winter, with storms blowing gale winds across the garden, hellebore flowers are tightly closed in bud, only 2 inches above the ground. The leathery leaves have taken the full brunt of the storm; bruised and battered around their edges, they collapsed, flat out, spent like broken whirligigs."

Hellebores are glorious awash in masses of violet-blue glory-of-the-snow. I've also interplanted them with early and midseason daffodils, species tulips, and snowflakes—a happy mingling.

PRIMROSES

Primroses (*Primula*) also look particularly nice sidling up to hellebores. They are such joyful flowers and there are so many different species that I decided to plant a primrose path. Perhaps I just liked the sound of Shakespeare's "primrose path of dalliance" or I'd read too many English novels, but to me a primrose path connotes a happy, carefree place to dally—definitely more rooted in my imagination than grounded in the garden. I chose a back path at the bottom of the woodland that I was in the process of clearing. It looped around the property edge and rejoined the path in the middle by the freestanding birdhouse. I planted a mixture of primroses—polyanthus, cowslips, hose-in-hose, and candelabra. In time my collection grew together to line the path.

The path grows in beauty and blooms over a 2-month period as each primrose increases in size. In January and February a few flowers bloom, nestled in their leaves for warmth. They don't look like much at first—whorls of inch-long leaves with flowers like polka dots peeking out. They are often caught blooming during a late snowstorm, yet take it in their stride and sit and wait before sending out more growth. As spring progresses, the flower stems lengthen, the number of blooms increases, and the leaves grow in heft and size.

The grand finale arrives in May and June, with the showy blooms of the Japanese primroses (*P. japonica*). They are aptly named the candelabra primrose because they hold their whorls of 8 to 12 flowers in tiers around 2-foot stems—first one tier blooms, then another starts a few inches above, then another, and another

Anticipation is one of the pleasures of gardening.

until five or more tiers have bloomed on each stem. The overlap of blooms lasts a month or more. The Japanese primroses bloom in primary colors—red, blue, and yellow—and in pastel colors—purple, pink, and peach. A colorful array will bloom for 6 to 8 weeks.

Most primroses increase by adding rosettes of foliage that can easily be teased apart. Spring is the best time to divide them. It is the wettest season and they won't dry out. One plant usually yields three and sometimes four or five rosettes that can bloom on their own when lifted, separated, and replanted. Their openhanded nature makes it easy to triple their numbers each year. In addition, each spring I find seedlings in the path, mostly polyanthus, which I round up and corral in the garden.

The real problem with my primrose path was not the primroses but its location. It led nowhere, and unless I deliberately chose to check on the flowers, I never walked that way. I missed the daily contact and probably many of the happier moments. So I decided to lift, divide, and move some of the plants nearer the house where I walk every day and where I could see them from a window in inclement weather.

I prepared a bed on one side of a pin oak near the driveway where I pass every day. Here, I planted the cowslip (*P. veris*). It is a wildflower that romps across the meadows and meanders through open English woods. I adore its modest beauty and its floppy clusters of nodding bells that are so sweetly scented. Because it is a vigorous grower and prefers drier conditions, unlike most other primroses, I figured it would be comfortable under a pin oak and perhaps would spread into the lawn. That hasn't happened. It has tightly filled its allotted space, which I continue to enlarge, and has circled the tree. *(continued on page 76)*

TOP, LEFT: Divide primroses by gently teasing apart the rosettes of foliage. TOP, RIGHT: The primrose path winds through the back of the woods. BOTTOM, LEFT: 'J. Barry Ferguson' primrose (*Primula veris* 'J. Barry Ferguson'). BOTTOM, RIGHT: English cowslip (*Primula veris*).

Chinese ground orchid
(*Bletilla striata*)

Snowdrops
(*Galanthus nivalis*)

Crown imperial
(*Fritillaria imperialis*)

Hellebore
(*Helleborus × hybridus*)

Yellow lady's slipper
(*Cypripedium calceolus*)

Checkered lily
(*Fritillaria meleagris*)

Lungwort (*Pulmonaria saccharata* 'Mrs. Moon')

Bloodroot
(*Sanguinaria canadensis*)

Virginia bluebells
(*Mertensia virginica*)

Daffodil 'Cheerfulness'
(*Narcissus* 'Cheerfulness')

As much as I liked this grouping, I still wanted a mixture of other varieties nearer the house. At the top of the wooded bank behind the house, I had been planting impatiens in the wake of tulips and hellebores. The impatiens had grown tiresome, and the border needed a face-lift, so I began adding clumps of primroses. The arrangement really took off, however, when our friend J. Barry Ferguson, a well-known horticulturist and floral designer, arrived with boxes of primroses he had dug up from his own garden. Barry had sold his house and was dismantling the garden. He brought the primroses to me for safekeeping, knowing that he could return and collect divisions without disturbing my planting.

One of the plants he brought me is named after him, the 'J. Barry Ferguson' primrose. The English call it a red hose-in-hose variety after an old custom of gentlemen pulling one stocking up to the thigh and another on top of it turned down just below the knee. One bloom does grow out from another, but I see it more as a trumpet-in-a-trumpet. Actually, it's a strumpet, the way it struts its stuff. No matter how many other primroses are nearby (including *Primula* 'Mark Viette', a true double with blooms that resemble small shocking pink roses with an old-rose fragrance to boot), this is the one that garners all the attention.

Most of the primroses Barry brought were the polyanthus varieties, the first to flower and the easiest to grow. Their wide range of colors and bicolors sparkle like precious stones in an overturned jewelry box, spilling out on the ground. They bloom in all the colors of the rainbow, large-eyed or clear-faced, in incredible combinations—navy blue and yellow, scarlet and cream, Wedgwood blue and pale yellow.

LUNGWORTS AND VIRGINIA BLUEBELLS

Lungwort (*Pulmonaria*) follows closely on the heels of the hellebores and blooms longer than the primroses. It pushes up its buds with its foliage and blooms when its first leaves are only an inch or so long. The flowers and the foliage then join forces, growing vigorously for 2 or 3 months before the flowers retreat, leaving the decorative foliage to continue on its own. During their long blooming period, the flowers change color from pink to blue, so in midseason a single plant bears a lively mix of the two. Many other lungwort cultivars are grown for their lung-shaped green leaves that are spotted, blotched, or streaked with white. They can be interplanted with a variety of early- to midseason bloomers—daffodils, snake's head fritillary, dwarf iris, grape hyacinth—in keeping with their size.

Foamflower (*Tiarella*) sends foaming white flowers a foot into the air and makes a better show if grape hyacinths are nearby to emphasize the purity of their bloom.

Virginia bluebells (*Mertensia virginica*) is another long bloomer that's almost a show in itself with flowers that open pink and then gradually brighten to a sapphire blue. It is easy to partner—a kerria in bloom encircled by Virginia bluebells is sensational. Combined with mid- and late-blooming daffodils or early tulips and snowflakes, it prolongs the spring party for 4 to 6 weeks. It behaves like a bulb rather than a perennial, quickly disappearing without a whimper after it blooms. By summer there is no trace of it.

Mayapples (*Podophyllum peltatum*) do the same. An accidental pairing placed them next to Japanese painted ferns. Each ran into the other's territory. Luckily, it worked out to everyone's benefit: The Mayapples disappeared shortly after the ferns sprouted, and the ferns didn't mind being hidden by a canopy for a month or so. There was never an empty space and never a complaint of crowding.

BLOODROOT AMONG THE ORCHIDS

Bloodroot (*Sanguinaria canadensis*), a perennial wildflower, is a particular favorite of mine. Like a child toting its blanket, the flower stands 6 inches high with a blue-green leaf—lobed, wavy, and kidney-shaped—folded in half around its head. It stays that way until the flower feels secure enough to lift its head and relax its leaf.

I have a lovely clump of lady's slippers (*Cypripedium calceolus*) that has thrived for more than a decade and is slowly on the increase. Last year I counted nine flowers, two joined together on one 2-foot stem. Their pouchlike flowers do resemble a lady's slipper held up for a garden Cinderella to try on.

Their flowers are designed as a sweet trap for insects, bees in particular. An insect enters the front opening and is prevented from exiting because of the inward-facing hairs. It must then negotiate an ingenious escape route in the course of which any pollen already on its body is rubbed off, and new pollen is picked up to deposit on the next flower.

Lady's slippers are mysterious creatures. They are difficult if not impossible for a gardener to grow from seed. The nutrients the seed needs to germinate come from a symbiotic relationship with a soil fungus. Then as the seedling grows, the fungus grows. It is found on full-grown lady's slippers. The symbiotic relationship

a garden vignette

I take great pride in my yellow lady's slippers, and yet I don't even know the name of the man who gave them to me. He worked for the company that installed our front gate, and more than a year later, on an afternoon when I was out, he generously deposited a few of these freshly dug wild orchids on my doorstep. He left word that he had been laying a foundation and had to disturb the lady's slippers. He thought that because we had so many gardens, we would give them a good home. I wish I could thank him personally.

The easy-to-grow Chinese ground orchid (*Bletilla striata* 'Albostriata') is a very desirable spring flower because its white pin-striped leaves are decorative even when there are no blooms.

is not fully understood, but it must help explain why the plants are so difficult to move and establish. That they have survived in my garden is dumb luck. I simply add a few inches of compost around them when they are dormant and keep any close intruders away. Each spring I bow down, gently stroke their leaves, and thank them for returning.

I am also proud of my **Chinese ground orchids** (*Bletilla striata* 'Albostriata'), although they are a cinch to grow. They're not as showy as the "ladies" but far more adaptable. Their flowers resemble those of a tender orchid with five loose petals surrounding a bottom tubular petal. The lavender-pink flowers are painted with dark stripes an inch across inside the throat. Each 1- to 2-foot stem has a spray of 6 to 10 flowers that open and bloom over a 6-week period; the narrow, pointed foliage is about a foot long with prominent lengthwise creases and a white pin-stripe edging each leaf. The cut flowers are long-lasting in arrangements, and the decorative foliage stays bright in the garden until after frost.

I ordered my original half-dozen from a Burpee catalog. Years later, I dug up one to move to another place along the path. It was shallowly planted and the earth was loose. I was surprised to pull up a string of a dozen bulbs, like a foot-long pearl necklace, running a few inches below the surface. From aboveground, it appeared the string of bulbs ended at what I had assumed was a separate plant. Only the bulbs at each end sent up flowering shoots. I broke them apart, replanted them separately, and each bloomed.

My curiosity got the best of me, and I dug up another Chinese ground orchid only to discover this time that the bulbs clustered together, rather than stretching out in a single line. Although I failed to learn why they formed this way, I did find out that technically they weren't bulbs at all, but pseudobulbs. Personally, I can't tell a pseudobulb from a bulb or a corm; and truthfully, I don't much care. It's more important to understand how it behaves. Surprisingly, several experts whose advice I respect recommend dividing a clump of Chinese ground orchids by thrusting a shovel into them. Rather than do this, which would slice up the bulbs, it seems better to use a spading fork, carefully lift a clump, gently pop them apart, and then replant. As long as they are attached to each other, many of the pseudobulbs can't be bothered to send up foliage and blooming stems. Broken apart and replanted, they have no choice but to perform. Ground orchids are not fragile and can be easily mixed in a bed with late-blooming bulbs—snowflakes, late daffodils, and wood hyacinths.

BLEEDING HEARTS AND LAVENDER MIST

Making themselves at home near the orchids, **bleeding hearts** (*Dicentra spectabilis*) boast graceful, 3-foot arching stems carrying heart-shaped flowers pendantlike above deeply cut, compound leaves. Each flower, to the delight of small children, is a perfect miniature valentine heart, puffy in bright pink or bride white.

The rapid growth of the plants is noticeable from day to day in spring. They are especially beautiful blooming in the midst of late-season tulips. In late summer they go dormant and die back to their roots to emerge once again in all their glory the following year. Their attractive ornamental foliage remains in good condition all summer if the plants receive enough moisture. If not, they go dormant early. In humus-rich, well-drained soil, the clumps grow fatter slowly and drop small presents of seedlings that can be transplanted to another part of the garden. I've never found them a nuisance.

One of my favorite accidental pairings that has been faithfully returning for a dozen years is bleeding hearts with peppermint-stick tulips. This tulip, one of the oldest in cultivation (dating to 1606 or earlier), has long, narrow white blooms striped with cheery red lines on 14-inch stems. It has naturalized to my bleeding hearts' content.

Lavender mist (*Thalictrum*) is a fitting name for the lacy, lavender-colored flowers that top these 4-foot skinny ladies. Despite their size, they are self-supporting and, when planted in clumps, make a wonderful backdrop for shorter bloomers. Placed singly at the front of a bed or along a path, they are so filmy that they don't block the view.

A Summer Respite

i find myself drawn to the woodland garden in the heat of summer most of all. A green garden like this has restorative and healing powers. It refreshes the spirit and cools the body. Around the ponds and at the edge of the woods, the morning sun spurs roses, hydrangeas, lotus, and water lilies into bloom. Daylilies colorfully follow the daffodils on the hillside, neither requiring much in the way of our attention.

Green and white dominate in early summer when clouds of white meadow rue and early blooming hosta light up the woodland path.

Yellow foxglove (*Digitalis grandiflora*) is a true perennial, warming the woodland with its glow early in summer and over and over again sporadically until fall frost.

Contrary to conventional wisdom, gardening in the shade, especially in mid-summer, is not an awkward nuisance but a welcome opportunity. A shady spot is an opportunity for a soothing garden. Luckily, every gardener has some shade, whether cast by a house, tree, shrub, arbor, fence, or garage. Most gardeners know that hostas, impatiens, and spring bulbs bloom in shade, but there are many other choices—shady ladies abound. It is perfectly possible, given some careful choosing, to have showy flowers and decorative foliage in shade through all gardening seasons—spring, summer, and fall.

A variety of shade-loving plants create a lush summer respite from the heat. Color sets a mood. Variegated foliage mimics nature's dappled sunlight, bringing more light into shady areas. The gold stripes on both *Hosta* 'Francis Williams' and *Hakonechloa macra* 'Aureola' are perfect choices. The golden ribbons of *H. macra* 'Aureola' hang dramatically to one side as if they had just been combed. It is the only grass I know that relishes shade. Yellow flowers—St. John's-wort (*Hypericum calycinum*), yellow foxglove (*Digitalis grandiflora*), and many columbines (*Aquilegia*)—add a cheery warm golden glow.

For a restful area, white is unbeatable—plants that wear white stay cool in summer. White flowers—*Hosta* 'Aphrodite' and fairy candles (*Actaea simplex*, formerly *Cimicifuga*), for example—act like beacons in the shade to draw your eye to them. Dark-colored plants—such as azure monkshood (*Aconitum carmichaelii*), blue

a garden vignette

I don't always strive for peace and quiet in shade. Near the small pond there is a solid mass of scarlet montbretia blooming among a sweep of Japanese blood grass. The effect is almost bloodcurdling. This is not a place to linger.

cardinal flower (*Lobelia cardinalis*), and lavender mist (*Thalictrum rochebrunianum*)—add depth and contrast. Foliage rarely draws attention to itself, but it can—a splash of red from Japanese blood grass is as invigorating as a cold shower.

Among the shade-loving plants, true perennial **foxglove** (*Digitalis grandiflora*) is an individual in more than one way. Its soft buttery yellow bells blend in easily with any other flower color. A clump-forming foxglove, it blooms first in early summer, then repeats all summer into late fall.

Totally adaptable **St. John's-wort** (*Hypericum calycinum*) produces sunny yellow 3-inch flowers no matter where it is placed—sun or shade, wet or dry conditions. After its full bloom in midsummer, a few flowers appear sporadically well into fall. I often plant it as a groundcover in a difficult site. The 18-inch stems of blue-green foliage darken to burgundy by first frost and hang on right through the toughest winters.

Foliage of Many Colors

Foliage combinations are restful when repeated. Too much variation can be unsettling, while some repetition binds the design together. The sheen of silvers in variegated foliage randomly hopping up the border, moving from foreground to center and back, takes your eye along for the ride. You don't always need to use the same plants, although that is a surefire way to start.

Choosing an edging for a flower border is a case in point. A ribbon of 'Gold Band' liriope can lead the eye down the path, its golden glimmers clearly drawing a line between the path and the plantings. An edging of silver-streaked liriope might be subtler and more restful, echoing the spiky blades of the lawn and blending in with the green foliage of many flowers. A clump of variegated Solomon's seal at the front of a bed draws the eye down the border, perhaps taking it deeper inside to a swath of silver liriope. This in turn might lead to another grouping of variegated euonymus climbing the trunk of a tree. A shrub of variegated Japanese andromeda at the back of the border glints silver.

I rarely plant fewer than three of one species in a single clump; usually, it's more—five, seven, perhaps a dozen. The smaller the plant, the more I cluster together. The small-fringed bleeding heart may be planted in clumps of a dozen, while only three hostas are enough to make a good showing. Odd numbers make it easier to weave one grouping of plants naturally into another. Sometimes the odd plant is placed in front of its neighbors, sometimes behind, thus imitating nature by suggesting colonization and spontaneous blending.

A tapestry of foliage

Confirmed flower lover that I am, I rarely plant a garden that depends purely on foliage and texture for effect. I design my sunny gardens around flower clusters. But one must accept that flowers are fleeting. Foliage arrives first and stays longer. In shade it is the foliage that weaves the plants into a pleasing tapestry of varying colors and shapes. Foliage can function both as the setting for passing clouds of bloom or as a star in its own right. As a visual fabric, foliage establishes a pattern, random or controlled. This fact is so obvious that I wonder why I didn't notice long ago.

Artists weave tapestries in two dimensions, but the art of gardening is more complex. It is a three-dimensional, constantly changing art form. A gardener partners plants to bring out the best in each. A plant is shown to best advantage when its textures and colors have something to play off of. Each leaf contrast emphasizes nature's diversity. Boredom gets a grip when too much of the same shape is repeated endlessly. A clump of a dozen hostas isn't as interesting as when hostas are mixed with other textures or when they serve as a backdrop for flowers. The elegant foliage of the fringed bleeding heart would be lost if placed next to a lacy fern. Its delicacy is emphasized when placed next to a broad-leaved perennial such as a hosta.

Most gardeners grow **hostas**—popular, indispensable plants for a shady garden. Using hostas can be a boring solution or an inspired one, depending on how they are employed. A mass planting of a single variety of hosta is often boring, although I successfully used one of the giant blue hostas to ring the huge trunk of a tulip tree. It called attention to the tree's girth, and there was nothing boring about the combination.

A cluster of a dozen hostas for no reason, however, is a blob. Conversely, a jumble of single specimens can be irritating to the eye. Having divided and moved my hostas many times, I find that weaving three, five, or seven of one kind into a group of a different variety is satisfying. The larger the hosta, the fewer needed. The same is true for other plants. Odd numbers make it easier to naturally weave groupings of plants together.

It is best to separate variegated plants with a solid-colored one. If you think about their genetic relationship, it makes sense. A blue hosta tinged with green could snuggle between a solid blue and a solid green—possible parents and an easy transition for the eye. I move them around in pots, standing back and checking the effect before I plant them.

The appeal of hostas is their wonderful array of foliage colors—blue, gold, green, and assorted variegated patterns. Their flowers are very much secondary and rarely a reason for planting them.

There are exceptions to this rule. If "beautiful" and "well mannered" define a lady, then *Hosta* 'Aphrodite', is one of the most elegant. It blooms with tall, double lilylike flowers. I have often fooled friends who see the flowers in bouquets and think I've located a deliciously perfumed unique, double lily. 'Royal Standard' and *H. plantagenea* are others with standout flowers.

Color, both of foliage and flowers, is the single most important element holding plant partnerships together. There may not be as many foliage colors as there are flower colors, but there are enough to create as lively a garden as one could possibly want.

Green, of course, is the dominant foliage color, but there are hundreds of shades of green in an array of fin-

ABOVE: The juxtaposition of assorted foliage—variegated and plain hosta, trillium, and *Epimedium*—creates a tapestry in the shade. OPPOSITE: The golden grass *Hakonechloa macra* 'Aureola' contrasts nicely with St. John's-wort.

ishes from glossy to matte and smooth to puckered. Add to this the sparkle from prisms of dew or glisten after rain when the glints of sunlight bounce back and forth. Green can be tinted with yellow, blue, red, purple, gray, or white. Some greens are not solid colors but blends and washes. Each notched leaf of the fringed bleeding heart (*Dicentra eximia*) is grass green bordered in lime green. Many hostas have blue-green or gray-green leaves. The blades of liriope are dark green.

Green used in a monochromatic design need not be dull if it is consciously manipulated for contrasting shapes, sizes, and textures. A combination of dark green bergenia backed by lime green ferns leaning over a blue-green hosta makes a cooling garden in the heat of summer.

i

The Final Fall Fling

n the cool of fall, the woods heat up again. The fiery color starts on the ground as the perennials die back and then ascends into the shrubs and the trees as their foliage turns. It is the year's final fling before the quiet of winter.

Some summer bloomers linger through fall and into winter, quietly changing colors as the flower petals dry.

Fall's final fling along the woodland path is a blend of changing foliage colors and late blooms such as fairy candles.

The birdhouse atop this pole was moved from the kitchen garden to the woodland, where it towers over the mop-head hydrangeas and hostas.

HYDRANGEAS

While some gardeners dream of giant flowers that bloom for months on end, others realize they can have that simply by planting hydrangeas. **Hydrangeas** (*Hydrangea*) are so adaptable, readily embracing full sun or shade, acid or lime soil. Shrubs with political aspirations, they change their flower color to fit the soil. If it is acid, the flower is blue; if alkaline, it is pink. A mophead perched above our pond must have one foot in acid soil and the other in alkaline—the flowers on one side are tinted with multiple shades of pastel pink, and on the other with purple and blue, rather like half-dipped Easter eggs. When aluminum sulfate is added to the soil every other week, gaudy blue flowers develop. For pinker flowers, add lime.

Hydrangea are not fussy as long as the drinks keep coming. In a hot, dry summer, the buxom bloomers do a lot of sulking, pathetically hanging their heads to their knees when they are thirsty, like spurned bar girls when no one is buying. When their thirst is quenched, however, their turgid stems rise up again, quickly recovering and rarely holding a grudge or showing a scar unless the drought is sustained. Experts flatly state hydrangea need no more water than other shrubs. That may be, but they certainly show the lack of water first. In my garden, I take their cry for help as a warning that other plants will follow if I don't turn on the sprinklers. I prefer them in shade where they are less trouble, look better, and are less likely to dry out. A soil enriched with leaf mold and dried manure holds moisture and gives them a nutritious diet.

Over the years I've collected mop-head, lace cap, and oakleaf hydrangeas. As members of the same family, they share a number of attractive traits, yet each has its own distinctive charm.

The bigleaf hydrangea (*Hydrangea macrophylla*) can be kept to shrub size—3 to 6 feet high with pruning—or left to grow to 10 feet with a similar spread. Depending on the variety, its flowers may be mop-heads or lace caps. The mop-heads remind me of pink or blue clouds of cotton candy. Each cloud is made up of clusters of 2-inch petals in a ball the size of a cantaloupe. The lace cap's blooms, by contrast, form doilies of lacy petals clustered and flattened together into giant blooms, each the size of a salad plate. After cutting some for dried flower arrangements, I deadhead those remaining back a few inches to the first bud. Conventional wisdom advises leaving the dried heads until spring to protect the buds, but the lace caps drop their blooms of their own accord in midwinter, and their buds are fine.

The oakleaf hydrangea (*Hydrangea quercifolia*), whose leaves resemble those of the red oak, is one of the most beautiful. The white flowers blush to a purplish pink in fall before drying to a golden brown in winter. Each cone-shaped panicle is a foot long. The oversize dark green leaves, up to 8 inches long, provide beautiful backdrops for the white flowers, especially when they turn a rich burgundy in fall.

While some gardeners dream of giant flowers that bloom for months on end, others realize they can have that simply by planting hydrangeas.

(The foliage of other hydrangeas usually turns yellow.) Oakleaf hydrangea grows 4 to 6 feet high and about as wide. As it ages, the roots spread outward, sending up new shoots to increase its spread. I grow two popular cultivars that light up the shade: 'Snowflake' and 'Snow Queen', one at the beginning of the path and one at the end. 'Snowflake' appears double, with multiple sepals arranged on top of each other. The large, heavy heads gently arch downward. 'Snow Queen' is not quite as heavily laden, but it does have more numerous florets than the species. It does double duty with an ornamental winter skeleton of rigid, reddish brown stems.

In fall, when the flower petals of the hydrangea feel papery to the touch, they can be picked and dried for winter bouquets. I hang them upside down in the dark, warm, dry attic for a few weeks so the stems dry straight. Bundles of mop-head blooms make a delightful dried-flower Christmas tree.

OTHER OUTSTANDING FALL PERENNIALS

Another key plant in the transition from late summer to fall is **Japanese anemone** (*Anemone japonica*). This is among our most beautiful shady ladies. Its single or double long-stemmed flowers dance in the breeze above dark green, deeply lobed foliage. They are long-stemmed and long-lasting as cut flowers.

A shade garden need not be subtle. It can manage sharp contrasts. Sometimes these may be found in a single plant, such as the **hardy begonia** (*Begonia grandiflora*), whose beautiful lime green foliage is veined blood red. The leaves loudly call attention to themselves as soon as they make their appearance in spring, yet they are not garish. Shaped like lopsided hearts, they fold slightly upward to reveal fiery undersides. Hardy begonias are among the last shade plants to bloom, waiting in the wings until October. When the flowers bloom atop the 2-foot stems, they start to make you think of Christmas. Even though the pink flowers are small, resembling those of the wax begonia, they are plentiful. The combined effect of leaves and blossoms is eye-catching from any point along the path. The decorative tan seedpods, like triangular puffed purses, sway on 3-foot stems long into winter.

Visually speaking, the ultimate shade plant may be **fairy candles** (*Actaea simplex*). In keeping with its common name, graceful 2- to 3-foot white flowers glow in the daytime shadows and the dusk of evening above 3- to 4-foot tall spikes. These narrow, tall plants form exclamation marks in the border.

Monkshood (*Aconitum*) resembles delphinium, but it is easier to grow. It blooms in early fall when few blue flowers are available to contrast with the changing foliage of shrubs and trees. Its dark blue hooded flowers closely cover the highest portion of each 4- to 5-foot stem. Beginning with a small clump purchased a decade ago, I have divided and replanted clumps every few years. They have naturalized along the driveway, at the back of the formal garden, and behind the house.

BELOW: The flowers of the toad-lily (*Tricyrtis hirta*) look like miniature orchids blooming along the stem.
OPPOSITE: Hydrangeas are water guzzlers and droop when they're thirsty. My lace cap hydrangeas bloom better when they are protected from the midday sun by the high canopy of a tree.

Common toad-lily (*Tricyrtis hirta*) apparently got its name from the coloration of its soft purple, orchid-shaped flowers that are blotched with dark purple, but I don't see it that way. Instead, I see the complex center of each bloom as a decorator's dream—a leopard-spotted orchid, no less. Each bud puffs up like a small purple balloon. All along the arching 2- to 3-foot stems, 3-inch flowers bloom individually, in pairs, or in triplets on short stalks. I pick toad-lilies for fall flower arrangements. These minutely detailed flowers demand up-close viewing to be fully appreciated.

I'm slightly in doubt about **hardy ageratum** (*Eupatorium coelestinum*), whose purple, shaggy, little button flowers closely resemble those of its popular annual cousin. Its pluses are its greater height, hardy constitution, shorter bloom time, drought resistance, yearly return, and ability to spread vigorously. Planted in a dry, shady corner, its tendency to roam is admirable—so far, I have welcomed it to other places along the path. Check back in a few years. I might think differently. It's a gardener's prerogative.

A Winter Wonderland

denuded of most of its foliage and bereft of color, winter does have its desolate days. It also has days of quiet beauty with sunlight bursting through the cathedral of bare branches and snow blanketing the ground, making the woods a wonderland.

Winter takes us back to the bare essentials, as if to remind us to appreciate fully what is to come. Without the austerity of winter, the other seasons would not be so spectacular.

A Japanese maple's sculptural beauty—the graceful umbrella of its bare branches—is a focal point in winter.

The real joy in winter lies in seeing what is hidden at other seasons. It's like being allowed into the dressing room to see the plants stripped to their essence and to grasp the working details: the sculptural beauty of bare branches, shaggy or silky barks, bird and wasp nests, leftover berries frozen in ice.

A little bare soil at this time of year is a good thing. It gives us a chance to witness the rebirth and renewal of the garden—the green noses of bulbs barely piercing the ground surface and the still-clinging seedheads and frost-blasted flowers. I enjoy the time.

The woodland walk has its particular pleasures in winter. Sculptures, benches, birdbath, and birdhouses define different areas of the walk in all seasons, leading the eye up the path, but they stand out more in winter as focal points. At the bottom of the path, the bright blue birdbath stops the eye, nudges it along to the birdhouse, and then leads it on to the tulip bench.

a garden vignette

At my house, plant labels regularly disappear. Either the lawn mower eats them or garden fairies move them around. The ones that stay tend to be unreadable. All this is complicated by the fact that my husband thinks labels make the garden look messy, so he pulls them up whenever he sees them. I agree, yet I want to keep track of what I've planted. Consequently, I've switched from using plastic and Magic Markers to etching names on copper tags and burying them at the base of the plants, where I can retrieve them (with a few scratches). As a backup, I write their names on my drawing of the garden and keep all the nursery receipts. I hope this will be a more lasting solution to repeated mysterious disappearances.

PLANTS WITH WINTER INTEREST

There are evergreens and conifers in coats of many colors—green, blue, gold, and silver—to brighten the dark days. They come into their own while the deciduous plants nap. English ivy, liriope, pachysandra, myrtle, and holly all contribute to the tapestry. Mix in the honey tones of epimedium, St. John's-wort, and black-leaved violets, and on fine winter days, there is much to enjoy on a woodland stroll.

Reds running toward purple appear in a few plants that hold onto their frost-colored foliage. One is **drooping leucothoe** (*Leucothoe fontanesiana*), whose arched branches support bronzed maroon leaves throughout winter. Variegated hybrids are also available.

A few **yaks** (*Rhododendron yakushimanum*), boasting shiny green flat leaves with silver underbellies, beg to be petted. *Nandina domestica*, topped with red berries, pleases the birds as much as it pleases us. **Oregon**

There is no need to hibernate for winter. There are

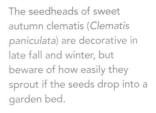

grapeholly (*Mahonia aquifolium*), whose musty-scented, lemon yellow flowers and leathery evergreen leaves are a dependable January special, have a double appeal, indoors and out—a budding branch cut in early winter can be brought inside to force. Once warmed, the buds open and pleasantly scent a room.

Japanese andromeda (*Pieris japonica*) is also evergreen and blooms with long drooping clusters of red, pink, or white bell-shaped flowers. The buds are set in fall and are colorful enough to mix with Christmas greens, even before they open in March or April.

Seeds and seedpods are important features of any garden in winter, especially a woodland garden. Tulip trees, sweet gums, and lindens all have decorative pods. Liriope holds its green foliage (and occasionally its black berries) all winter; depending on the severity of the cold, the tips and a portion of the green blades may brown, but they are still attractive when little else is green.

The seedheads of sweet autumn clematis (*Clematis paniculata*) are decorative in late fall and winter, but beware of how easily they sprout if the seeds drop into a garden bed.

Plants that alter as they go through the seasons emphasize the mutability of natural things. This can be as simple as contrast between the rich burgundy blush of the foliage that perks up the azaleas and the green ivy at their feet. The clumps of **Miscanthus sinensis 'Variegatus'** never look better than when the seedheads have turned a glowing almond color after repeated frosts and sparkle with a dusting of snow. The cold brings out the translucency of their blades as sunlight dances through them.

Even through the bleak winter months, this ornamental grass often retains much of its volume to fill the space. Last winter, however, the first heavy snow knocked it flat. I assumed it was a goner. But no sooner had I turned my back than it rose up again, as sturdy as before. I had assumed the brown dried stalks were easily broken. Yet over winter they battled repeated snows and high winds successfully. There is much to admire in ornamental grasses.

There is no need to hibernate for winter. There are always wonders to behold while you are waiting for spring flowers.

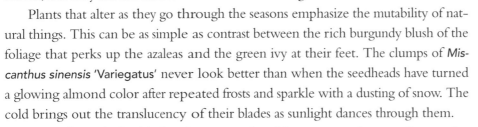

wonders to behold while you are waiting for spring flowers.

The Formal Flower Garden

June is my favorite month for visitors. The abundance of flowers is overwhelming. Our formal flower garden and the crescent rose garden at the southern end of it have their moments of greatest glory, with the

In early June, the flower garden is a swath of blues and purples, with catmint lining the edge, columbines in the middle, alliums popping up in back, and a tree lilac blooming outside the wall.

splendor of the flowers hiding any mistakes or inadequacies. It is a different story in July and August, when I am forced to look elsewhere for excuses — the weather, the bugs, the humidity, the neighbor's dog.

this garden is on the south side of the house and faces a large covered porch where our family sits and reads on summer weekends and dines on balmy evenings. In 1978, when we first moved in, the only things you saw looking south were three craggy old apple trees, precariously balancing themselves on dead branches the way an elderly gentleman is supported by a cane. They bore little, if any, fruit. For years we steadfastly gazed the other way toward the bay, ignoring them. Finally, one tree died, and we realized that the others were liabilities. With their departure, we had sudden visions of long flower borders with roses at the end in their place. It was then that we called on Alice Recknagel Ireys and, inspired by her expertise, our gardening turned serious.

Lunch in the garden under the shade of the linden tree is a favorite summer activity. The branches hold a flowering chandelier of hydrangeas and candles for evening suppers.

The Garden's Structure

the land was far from flat. It sloped gradually, losing 8 feet in altitude from the porch before reaching a bluff overlooking the bay. Alice designed a large, level bluestone terrace off the porch to make entertaining and hosting events such as a wedding easy. She lined both sides of the area that would become the long flower borders with 78 feet of 4-foot-high stucco walls that match the siding of the house. The walls protect the garden from the salt air and high winds. They also divide it from more informal areas, adding a bit of privacy.

At the far end of the parallel walls, we built a curved retaining wall to hold the 3 feet of soil needed to level the garden and to link the beds. We planted a holly hedge on top to enclose this end of the garden and to stop strong winds from staging races through the roses. For easy access, we positioned gates opposite each other at the southern end and a third one off the driveway on the north end. The

Diversity, I quickly discovered, is the basis of a better garden.

side of the terrace facing the bay was left open for the sake of the view. Midway between the garden gates, Alice designed a reflecting pool with a small fountain.

When the walls first went up, the place looked like nothing so much as a prison yard, and I began to lose heart. But then truckloads of topsoil and compost arrived. We drew the borders—literally pouring ground limestone from a pitcher as if it were paint—undulating out 8 to 12 feet and back again three times along each wall. Each border was a mirror image of the other. We left 2 feet at the back of each border along the wall unplanted and mulched the area with wood chips so as to make it easier to weed or prune without stepping into the bed. (Once the quick spurt of spring growth begins, the plants hide this pathway.) With 500 perennials placed in the borders and sod laid between the beds, the garden looked much better.

A month later, plants were dying in droves. We quickly realized that we had a serious drainage problem. It was a tough way to learn that drainage is of huge importance. I had gladly planted all those perennials myself, and now, sadly, I dug them up, heeling them in on the far side of the wall while workers laid three drainage pipes along the length of each border. This time I hired help to replant;

OPPOSITE: Tall hollyhocks blooming outside the formal garden peek over the wall and appear to be blooming inside the garden, adding to its lushness.

I couldn't face it alone. Yet the setbacks, the huge expense, and the unexpected labor only made us realize more than ever how much we wanted this garden. Our resolve turned out to be justified. With a year of nurturing, we could see the possibilities: The beauty of the plants was evident, although the garden still needed tweaking and the walls were too much in evidence.

ADDING CLEMATIS AND CLIMBING ROSES

During the first few years, we managed to cover the walls with **sweet autumn clematis**—a quick fix. Capable of running 20 to 30 feet in a season, it grew up and over the walls unstoppably. The white fluffy blooms puddled like whipped cream on top of the wall in a delightful way, and the vanilla perfume wafted to different parts of the garden. The seedpods look like golden balls spun from silken thread. These fine threads help the seeds to ride the wind to new areas of the garden, where they plant themselves.

When I first introduced sweet autumn clematis, I had no idea that it readily self-seeds and would, if given half a chance, strangle the tall perennials at the back of the

border. Now I rigorously pull up seedlings and root out surplus vines in winter. They are sneaky. Once the plants sprout, they are hard to find until they creep up the wall again. In that case, I let them bloom. While fastidious gardeners will cut them back before they seed, I admit that I often miss this stage by not watching closely enough. But I don't want to eliminate them, only control them. Because sweet autumn clematis grows less vigorously in shade, I tend to leave it at the shady end of the beds and cut it to the ground each winter.

As the wall went up, I planted a dozen large-flowered clematis, but none survived. Wilt killed a few and dry soil got the others. Wilt can't easily be prevented; unfortunately, its cause is not understood. But if a ripe (not green) clematis stem is planted 6 inches deep, it can send up new shoots after being attacked by wilt. In my experience, once it battles wilt and survives, it doesn't suffer again. As for the drought, I didn't know then that cement sucks up moisture like a sponge. I had planted too close to the wall. I now plant clematis 3 feet out from the wall and direct them to climb up wires or up the bare legs of climbing roses.

I have tried pruning clematis but found it a mostly thankless job. For pruning purposes, clematis are divided into three groups, and each group is supposed to be

OPPOSITE: 'Cecile Brunner', 'Cornelia', and 'Dr. Van Fleet' roses bloom over the walls at the back of the garden. Pinks and lady's mantle sprout at the front, while foxgloves and *Nectaroscordum siculum* bloom in the middle.
ABOVE, LEFT: 'Zephirine Drouhin' rose is a blooming background for wild indigo (*Baptisia australis*).
ABOVE, RIGHT: 'Zephirine Drouhin' climbs the pillar with lamb's ears and *Veronica teucrium* 'Crater Lake Blue' at her feet.

dealt with in a different way. Suffice it to say, I no longer give the matter much thought or attention. I find that clematis do as they want anyway and fussing is unnecessary. In spring, after they leaf out, I remove any noticeable dead stems. That's about it. Aside from my cutting flowers for arrangements, my clematis go their own way.

We placed wooden trellises at each pillar along the wall for the **climbing roses**, but the roses quickly outgrew them. So we stretched 4-foot lengths of strong wire horizontally between eyebolts at 1-foot intervals up the wall, adding more spans as the roses grew higher and tying the canes loosely to the wires with twine. This supported the roses, and the clematis grabbed hold of either the wires or the roses by themselves.

Climbing roses soon became a glorious obsession with us. Eventually, we had roses outside the walls climbing in and inside the walls climbing out. They often hooked together at the top, so no tying up was needed.

One of the first climbing roses to bloom over the wall was 'Dr. Van Fleet'. It was striking all through June with a fashionable boa of purple 'Jackmanii' clematis twisting through it. But then it was finished for the year, and I was greedy for more blooms. I replaced the doctor with 'New Dawn', a semidouble pink rose, long-limbed and ever-blooming. Having previously grown 'New Dawn' over the kitchen garden arbor and on the side of the house, I knew it wouldn't disappoint me.

Climbing roses soon became a glorious obsession with us.

Across the way, I planted the fiery red rose 'Don Juan'. The tall perennials at the back of the garden hide its summer slump. If a plant has a recurring condition that doesn't hurt its bloom or endanger its life, I hide it rather than treat it with chemicals. What can't be seen can't hurt!

'Zephirine Drouhin', a shrieking pink climber, grows at the southern end on the pillar. Probably looking for attention, as women are wont to do, Zeph climbed over the wall and up the lilac tree on the other side. It is another accident I am happy to take credit for. The lilac tree, a 'Miss Kim' standard, blooms late as lilacs go, and the rose is one of the earliest, so their displays overlap. 'Zephirine Drouhin' sporadically flowers over summer and into fall, giving the lilac blossoms when it has none of its own. The clematis 'Niobe' follows on the heels of the rose to top the lilac, embroidering both with its flowers.

Noticing how the beds inside the garden claimed blooms from outside the walls—the crab apple, the lilac tree, the shrub roses—I planted white **hollyhocks** along the outside of the walls to lend height and still more blossoms to the garden within. Now as the first flush of the roses fades, hollyhocks are the garden's glory. Their huge single flowers with natural pearlescence are positively radiant basking in the glow of the setting sun. Peering like friendly neighbors over the fence to share a bit of fun, they use their position to advantage—the wall hides their inevitable rusty bottoms.

CHASTE TREES BRING ON THE BLUES

The original design inside the borders called for anchoring each end with a **chaste tree** (*Vitex agnus-castus*) to add substance and to balance the flimsy perennial flowers. They are still there, when almost every other detail of the original planting design has changed.

I thought I'd lost them the second year. Chaste trees, it turns out, are late risers. As late as the end of May, when every other plant has leafed out, they still look dead, with not a sprout of green anywhere. Then they miraculously put on a couple feet of growth in June and again in July and August. These bare stubs leave a gaping hole in spring, so to camouflage the problem, I planted clematis 'Nelly Moser', a large-flowered early bloomer, at their feet. She gussies them up until the foliage appears.

Chaste tree leaves are dark green above and silvery gray underneath and shimmer attractively in a gentle breeze even before the blooms appear. Each winter I severely prune the plants to keep them shrub size, so that the blossoms are near the ground. (I could have let them grow into trees, in which case no regular pruning would be necessary.) I leave the two growing in shade at the north end of the garden at 3 feet high; I cut the ones in the sun to only 1 foot because they grow faster in the open. By August, they are all the same impressive size—8 feet high and 6 feet wide. Their baby-powder sweet, lilac blue flowers form along terminal heads. New flowers continue opening until October, and the shrubs are dressed from top to bottom, usually accessorized with butterflies.

I save the chaste tree prunings. They are strong, flexible, fairly thin, and honey-colored—most useful for making twig fences and staking perennials without detracting from the plants as bamboo or metal stakes do. Many of the branches grow in wishbone shapes, making it easy to push the handle into the ground to support a plant or to weave the branches into a bean fence with overlapping twigs in the kitchen garden (see page 50). By summer's end, approximately one in six of the sticks stuck in the ground has rooted and even bloomed. I transplant the rooted stems to a place behind the lilac and peony walk, thus adding bloom in late summer when the walk is otherwise a mix of quiet greens.

The Perennial Dilemma

We chose perennials for bloom from late April until October, the months we spend our leisure time outside on the porch rather than in the living room. The palette of color started out with soft pinks, blues, and purples. A few whites worked their way in, a touch of red, too, but yellow and orange are never permitted. I once added dwarf yellow lilies, thinking the contrast might add some sparkle, but the gesture failed. Yellow dominates the kitchen garden and lights up the woodland walk, but it didn't work here. The yellow lilies flamed rather than sparkled and interrupted what we wanted: a restful garden with soft colors that reflected the sun during the day and the moon at night.

As now established, the perennial show begins in late April when the first blossoms—a few tulips and columbine—appear along with the pink double blossoms of the crab apple on the other side of the wall. By May, you would think that the plants were on growth hormones, their foliage sprouts so quickly. The first blooms are mostly blues and pinks—columbine, dianthus, salvia. By the end of May and early June, the garden is moving full steam ahead, well into one of its magical moments. The tall blue spikes of lupines and the pink, purple, and crimson foxgloves brighten the middle of the border, while roses in all their splendor bloom extravagantly at the far end in the crescent border and over the walls.

July can be sleepy. The heat makes us all lethargic. Plant growth slows to a snail's pace. It is pleasant enough, just lacking oomph, until the blue and white balloon flowers burst, the lilies trumpet their arrival, and the purple *Verbena bonariensis* spikes the air. Oomph returns in spades in August, when the bloom on the chaste trees complements the bloom of the summer phlox. It wanes slightly in September but ends with a bang—the season's grand finale—in October, when deep blue monkshood, rosy sedum 'Autumn Joy', and the ruffled bright aster 'Harrington's Pink' share the limelight. From the first bloom to the last, the garden is a shifting symphony of fragrance, shape, color, and texture.

Many of our first settlers are gone, which is perfectly normal in a garden's development. Every garden, no matter how well designed, needs regular plant

The formal garden has a succession of blooms from spring through fall. TOP, LEFT: Late April features tulips and lilacs. TOP, RIGHT: Late May finds pinks, Oriental poppies, and wild indigo in bloom. BOTTOM, RIGHT: Early June stars alliums, iris, and salvia. BOTTOM, LEFT: Sedum 'Autumn Joy' and asters share the limelight in late October.

shuffling and reshuffling as tastes change and plants die or overstep their bounds (sometimes bringing about the demise of others) and need to be rooted out.

Trial and error is an indispensable process. Even individual plants benefit. Searching out the most suitable garden phlox, a family susceptible to mildew, I gradually eliminated the vulnerable ones during the first few years, replacing them with new varieties until those that remain are very mildew-resistant. I haven't been bothered with that problem for years.

Lackadaisical plants were discarded as new flowers caught my fancy; finicky perennials departed on their own—coral bells, candytuft, and delphiniums among them. Meanwhile, aggressive varieties have taken up more space. The garden's border as designed was intended to have groups of half a dozen coral bells alternating with candytuft. Neither plant liked it here. I finally put other plants in their stead. Now informality reigns. I've learned that the plants in one border won't grow the same way as those in the other. Even a small distance of 30 feet can make a difference, so although the plantings may be the same, they do not match. The two borders now mirror each other only in shape.

Clumps of assorted perennials alternate around the curves—astilbe, dianthus, lady's mantle, lamb's ear, and catmint dominate. The edges do not restrict the plants; many spill over, softly blurring the lines. In the case of plants like blue columbine, *Verbena bonariensis,* foxglove, and an occasional blue lupine, self-seeding is rife. A few blooms flourish in new places every year. Mingling among neighboring flowers, they relax the strong lines of the garden. The borders are, in fact,

a garden vignette

Decades of gardening have taught me that the garden contains more instruction than a library. Often the plants themselves show me simple solutions to problems I haven't solved. Clematis 'Henryi' languished for several years on a trellis at the back of the border, hardly able to lift itself to the top of the wall. I'd help it up one day, twisting it through a slat, and it would flop back down the next. Nothing I did kept it up. It finally received help from the 'American Pillar' climbing rose growing on the other side of the wall that had reached over and down, gently curving out from the wall, enabling the clematis to twine around it and clamber up. That's when I decided to add climbing roses on the inside of the wall to complement the ones on the outside.

merely skeletons with meat on their bones. There are no blobs of color but rather waves of blooms that gently crest over and into each other.

Annual Accents

the garden was designed as a perennial garden at a time when, I must admit, I turned up my nose at annuals. Annuals just seemed too common, too ordinary. Of course, come midsummer, when those much-adored perennials were waning and my borders cried out for color, my garden snobbery did an about-face. I ran to the local nursery for a few long bloomers—blue salvia, heliotrope, and nicotiana. Diversity, I quickly discovered, is the basis of a better garden. As far as annuals are concerned, I now have no prejudices or petrified opinions. After all, many of the annuals I may plant to plug holes are perennials in a climate milder than ours. Besides, a plant with a pretty face is always hard to resist. Plenty of them have been welcomed into my garden without too many inquires about their habits or manners.

Rosa 'American Pillar' reaches up, over, and into the garden from outside the wall to lend a helping hand to clematis 'Henryi' to climb.

Of course, the behavior of plants is often not easy to assess before you grow them yourself. Catalogs and books try to be definite, but soil and weather can make an unpredictable difference. A plant that's invasive in a mild climate is often restrained where winters are cold. A rampant grower in the sun can be a pussycat in the shade—that is, if it is shade-tolerant and grows at all. Many plants have an extraordinary tolerance for a wide range of conditions. On many occasions, I have pushed the limits and had surprisingly good results.

Choosing a plant is a bit like screening a job applicant—it's easy to be fooled. It may take a year or two before I know whether the plants I purchased crawl, walk, run, leap, or blindly charge ahead, knocking down everything in their way. **Musk mallow** (*Malva moschata*) deceived me for a decade until I awoke one sunny day to realize that this shy little creature had self-seeded itself all the way down the border, filling every gap and hole with hollyhock-like, satiny, soft pink, 2-inch flowers carried on 3-foot branching stems. Those subtle blooms never drew much attention to themselves, serving instead as filler, softly *(continued on page 112)*

Darwin hybrid tulip
(*Tulipa* 'Apeldoorn')

Clematis 'Nelly Moser'
(*Clematis* 'Nelly Moser')

Vervain
(*Verbena bonariensis*)

Peacock orchid
(*Gladiolus callianthus*)

Lamb's ear
(*Stachys byzantina*)

Oriental hybrid lily
(*Lilium*)

Hollyhock
(*Alcea rosea*)

Balloon flower
(*Platycodon grandiflorus*)

Allium
(*Allium aflatunense*)

Columbine 'Nora Barlow'
(*Aquilegia* × *hybrida* 'Nora Barlow')

uniting other plants. I spent a few hours removing the ones that had ventured too far, as well as those crowding more valuable plants. Now I'll leave them alone for a few years or so, until they catch my eye again.

Fool's onion (*Triteleia laxa* 'Queen Fabiola') blooms up through the flowering skirts of lady's mantle.

Gooseneck loosestrife (*Lysimachia clethroides*) is another matter entirely. As noted earlier, you need to weed it out each spring to keep it under control. **Verbena bonariensis** self-seeds, but it does so in close clumps. It is a slim Jim of a plant, standing tall and narrow. It doesn't block the view of anything behind it. I planted it at the front of the border, where a ground hugger is usually expected. The arrangement playfully breaks up the monotony of the edging.

A Boost from Summer Bulbs

In my never-ending quest for more flowers, summer bulbs of all kinds have been pressed into service and are nestled under, around, and between the perennials. This is nature's way. Any plant that sleeps for most of the year must share a room. So fool's onions, assorted alliums, peacock orchids, and lilies poke up through the foliage of various perennials, adding more bloom. Some have been layered like spring bulbs under the skirts of perennials. The result is more flowers in the same space.

FOOL'S ONIONS

In early summer **fool's onion** (sold as both *Triteleia laxa* 'Queen Fabiola' and *Brodiaea laxa* 'Queen Fabiola') playfully jostles among the low growers at the front of the border. When its blue flowers embrace the chartreuse flowers of lady's mantle, they both twinkle happily. The blooms, falling galaxies of inflorescences up to 6 inches across, are made up of 12 to 15 deep violet tubular flowers that flare into stars on symphony of fragrance, shape, color, and texture.

2-foot stems. Fool's onion actually belongs to the lily family. Frequently, its leaves die back before the flowers are fully open, making the plant easy to tuck under the foliage of another plant. Plant the bulbs 5 inches deep and they will generate cormels, or offsets. Inexpensive, easy to grow, easy to naturalize in sun or part shade, and long-lasting in bouquets—what's not to like about fool's onion? Yet it is not often grown. It should be. I have found that the plants faithfully return, increasing in number over the years. Fool's onion minds its manners and doesn't leave a mess on departure.

ALLIUMS

Members of the *Allium* family, or **true onions**, are more than pretty faces. Reputed to repel vampires, they work like a charm when planted into the garden. Van Engelen, a highly respected bulb catalog, lists 30 different kinds, and I'm on my way to planting them all. Be assured that while the bulbs smell like onions, once planted, their odor stays in the ground. (However, if you crush the leaves, you'll get a whiff, but why would you do that?)

The first allium to bloom is blue garlic (*A. caeruleum*). I layered a clump under a mat of catmint. The cornflower blue balls of the garlic, bobbing atop 2-foot stems, contrast nicely with catmint's floppy purple plumes. Because it was so happy snuggling under the catmint, I tucked *A. cowanii*, another diminutive bloomer with clusters of the whitest, glistening flowers, under another clump. I encourage both to seed where they like.

Following close behind is *A. siculum,* or rather *Nectaroscordum siculum,* as it now prefers to be called. Botanists recently gave it its own genus. A coup indeed! I don't know what the plant did to deserve it, but as far as gardeners are concerned, it acts like, smells like, and looks like a flowering onion, so that's how I treat it.

I plant *Nectaroscordum* in the middle of the border because its 3- or 4-foot stem never needs staking and has no trouble supporting 20 to 30 nodding bells. Sometimes it does take an impish turn and crawls along the ground before curving up and arching into a lazy S. Each green bell has a reddish tinge and is slightly less than an inch in length and width. The bells stay for

Oriental lilies love to have their bottoms in the shade of vitex with their heads peeking out between the flowering branches.

weeks, hanging their heads in bloom. Once fertilized and turning to seed, the pedicels stand proudly erect, like blushing brides empowered by the loss of virginity. The seedheads have their own charm, drying to a pale parchment. I let them stand in the garden until I tire of them. One tug and the stems easily detach from the bulb, leaving the long, fleshy, strap-shaped leaves to die back. The leaves are easy to ig-

Choosing a plant is a bit like screening a job applicant—it's easy to be fooled.

nore—they stay close to the ground and are hidden by the perennials in front of them. Clumps have increased over the years, and I move the surplus into other places.

A. aflatunense and some of its inexpensive hybrids, such as 'Gladiator', 'Lucy Ball', and 'Purple Sensation', are so dependable that they dominate the early show when their 4-inch dense spheres of starry lilac-to-purple flowers sway atop 3-foot stems. The strap-shaped foliage kindly departs when the flowers begin to bloom and doesn't distract from their glory. The flowers remain decorative for months, fading slowly from purple to silvery gray and on to light honey tones, drying naturally in the garden. A few I pick for summer bouquets, and the rest stay until fall, when they move indoors in dried bouquets and Christmas decorations.

The drumstick alliums find their place near the middle of the border. They bloom in early July for 2 to 3 weeks, a relatively quiet time in the garden, after the roses peak and the lupine and foxglove are cut back. Nothing can compete with them. Shaped like bass drumsticks, they have 2-inch oval flower heads, each fully packed with 50 to 100 reddish purple blossoms. Even before their green flowering buds open in late June or July, they are decorative—afterward, too, as they dry and fade to tan.

PEACOCK ORCHIDS

The delightfully scented **peacock orchid** (*Acidanthera bicolor*, also *Gladiolus callianthus*) behaves like a gladiolus. It must be planted out each spring and taken in each fall in our climate. But in summer the white flowers on 3-foot stems are magnificent, splashed with deep purple centers; in a gentle breeze, they look like great butterflies swaying above sword-shaped leaves. The peacock orchid is an inexpensive bulb—two dozen for less than $5—and deserves to be better known. A dozen or more grouped in the middle of the border bloom for more than 2 months as the flowers open continuously on individual stems from the bottom up. They are too full-bodied and too shallowly planted to be layered under other plants; they really need their own space. I plant them in front of 'Harrington's Pink' asters because they bloom first, before the asters spread their elbows out and lean heavily over everything nearby.

LILIES

Because Oriental lilies grow straight up on a single, scantily clad stem, they take up little room in the garden. And the bulbs, deeply planted to 6 to 8 inches, leave room for perennials above them. Luckily, too, lilies prefer to have their ankles shaded by the skirts of perennials or shrubs while their heads enjoy the sun. I've paired Orientals such as 'Star Gazer', a crimson outlined in white, with blue-flowered vitex to very happy effect. They nudge out between the vitex branches like children playing peekaboo.

Normally, I'm pretty conventional and put lilies where their height is in keeping with that of their neighbors, but every now and then I throw convention to the wind and place several near the front of a border. Standing there in lonely splendor, they appear all dressed up and out for a stroll.

Standing there in lonely splendor, lilies appear all dressed up and out for a stroll.

Visitors for some reason assume that these beds inside the walls are the highest-maintenance gardens. Yet once they were planted and the plants filled in, they never demand weekly care. I do regularly deadhead favorite plants, pinching them off at the neck—balloon flowers, in particular—to keep them blooming. I weed the beds fewer than half a dozen times a year, generally in early spring or late winter, again in midsummer and late summer, and occasionally in late fall. A month or more may pass during the bloom season during which no weeding is done, and the garden still looks presentable. I plant closer together than is usually advised; this encourages plants to send their roots deeper rather than wider and shades out weeds. Of course, when we have a lot of visitors and my reputation is on the line, you'll find me out there weeding like anything.

From diamonds to dump trucks

There are times in a woman's life, especially that of longtime mothers, when a special gift lights up her life. For some, it's diamonds; for me, It was a dump truck.

An addiction to gardening can drive a person to extraordinary lengths. For years I had been casually mentioning how convenient it would be to have such a vehicle—usually after I was caught transporting a tree or a large shrub in the front seat of my husband's car with the top sticking out of the sunroof. But I still didn't expect to get one.

From the moment the GM dump truck arrived, my life changed dramatically. On my first outing with a gardening friend, we decided to make a day of it and stop for lunch along the way to the nursery. Parking for lunch is not easy in a dump truck—we ended up at a truck stop. Even there, space was tight, so while I went in for sandwiches, she stayed with the truck.

When I returned with the food, the truck was surrounded by men, and my friend was demonstrating its dumping capabilities. "Wow,"

I thought, "single women, take notice." In fact, the men only had eyes for our bright, new, state-of-the-art truck. Now that it has put on a few years of hard use, no one notices it—or us—anymore.

From that first day, I have instinctively known how many plants the truck will hold. It makes no difference whether I'm buying annuals in spring, planting an island of shrubs in fall, or designing a new garden for a friend. The plants I assemble fill the truck completely, with almost always one left over for my lap.

In addition to the money saved picking up free compost from the town heap, free manure from horse farms, and wood chips from landscapers, I avoid all delivery charges from the local nurseries. The truck makes it easier to buy more plants at one time, saving gas on return trips, and we can unload it at our leisure at home. Of course, it goes without saying that I buy more plants than I might otherwise.

I may not be the envy of the other women on the block, but the freedom that comes from owning my own dump truck is compensation enough.

My dump truck has proved invaluable to our gardening enterprise.

The Formal Rose Garden

The formal rose garden has great bones. Its crescent shape is defined by a holly hedge in back and a dwarf boxwood edging in front. These give the garden substance year-round, even in winter when we look right through

This summer rose bouquet includes apricot 'Abraham Darby', red 'Don Juan', and striped 'Fourth of July' roses, along with blue lupines and white-and-pink sweet Williams.

the naked rose canes. The holly's evergreen foliage and red berries appear to come forward as the dark green of the boxwood recedes, looking lush from a distance.

As originally designed, the garden held modern roses—90 hybrid teas, two grandifloras, 4 polyanthas, 6 shrub roses, and another half-dozen standards. I dutifully sprayed weekly and waged war on every attacking insect—Japanese beetles, aphids, you name it. Some days the smell of chemicals hung so heavy in the air that I couldn't smell the roses. But despite my ministering to their every whim, they still looked pretty dismal by midsummer. I was a nurse in a war zone, not a gardener. At the same time, my awareness of the harm chemicals do to the environment was increasing as were the demands of my four children. I finally went cold turkey on the chemical addiction.

O ver the next few years, a number of the hybrid teas departed on their own. I threw out the others with the trash. The two grandiflora roses, both 'Queen Elizabeth', held their thrones regally, one on each side. I hadn't the heart to prune them down. They were glorious towers of bloom and scent and still are to this day. By June they're 6 feet high and often peak at 8 feet before winter. Each is backed by two squat 'The Fairy' polyanthas that insist on growing wider than tall. Large clusters of clear pink pompoms smother the branches from early summer until late fall. In the center the six 'Sea Foam' shrub roses have grown together into one large bush. It is the last rose to bloom, starting in mid- to late June as the May bloomers are waning. The buds are deep pink, opening to a soft pink, and then whiten as they age. Our current

mix of early-, mid-, and late-blooming cultivars assures us 2 glorious months of roses blooming full out before they doze, with some sporadic bloom in July and August. In September we get a second flush, but it doesn't compare to the earlier bloom.

I've refilled the space vacated by hybrid teas and standards with English, antique, and shrub roses. We have all heard tales of "rose sickness," supposedly the result of planting a rose where another had grown. Judging from my experience, this is hogwash—an example of the kind of broad statements, half-truths, and lies perpetuated in the literature of rose care.

When I plant a rose, even where there was a rose before, I simply add compost, topsoil, and cow manure to each hole. As long as the soil is enriched each year, the roses do fine. Roses are heavy eaters and drinkers, exhausting a soil if it is not replenished yearly. A depleted soil does not grow good roses. Rose ads imply that a chemical fertilizer is all that is needed, but without organic matter, a fertilizer is useless (see page 28). David Austin, the famous English rosarian who breeds my favorite group of roses, agrees. *(continued on page 124)*

At the entrance to the formal rose garden, *Rosa* 'Scarlet Meidiland' blooms on one side with *Rosa rugosa* on the other.

So although the roses are the center of it is the chorus line of other bloomers

attention in this garden,
that helps their beauty shine.

Two years ago I had the privilege of having lunch with David at his garden, and we discussed such things at length. When he began to breed roses, his aim was to capture their lost scents. He has been wildly successful in this and in producing multiple petals in modern roses at the same time, improving their vigor, repeat bloom, and disease resistance. Repeat bloomers have only been around for a little more than a century; considering that roses are one of our earliest garden plants, that isn't much.

David backcrosses modern roses to old roses, unlike most other breeders who cross modern roses with other new roses. Despite the unpredictability of the process, David has bred some of the most fragrant roses ever known. Each year, about 150,000 crosses are made from 200 to 300 parent roses. Of the 600,000 seeds collected and immediately planted in September and October, approximately one-third germinate.

I found it surprising that roses grown from seed flower 6 or 7 months after planting. It seemed worth a try in my own garden until he explained that only 5 or 6 out of every 250,000 seedlings are deemed keepers. The selected ones are then budded onto vigorous rootstock and planted out in fields, where they are observed over the next 8 or 9 years. (Recently, David has started growing more roses on their own rootstock. This will probably be an important improvement in the future.)

His rigorous approach—assessing field-grown roses for their foliage, shape, range, and clarity of flower color; repeat bloom; and fragrance two or three times a week for several months, at different times of the day, then ruthlessly destroying all but the top five or six for final introduction—has paid off. The time between planting the seed of the first cross to a new introduction takes a minimum of 8 years. Since 1961, he has introduced approximately 150 cultivars.

The English roses may be single, semidouble, or fully packed into cup shapes, domes, or rosettes—all quite different from the high-pointed, nose-in-the-air blooms of the hybrid tea. To match the blooms, English roses have a natural shrubby form with none of the stiffness of the other   *(continued on page 128)*

A floral foam frame is soaked in water, then covered with pachysandra before fool's onion and an of assortment roses, including 'Eden', 'Scarlet Meidiland', and 'The Fairy' are poked in.

I admit that I'm bewitched by roses and

I aim to please them.

Rosa
'Bonica'

Rosa
'Golden Wings'

Rosa
'Abraham Darby'

Rosa
'Ballerina'

Rosa
'Heritage'

Rosa
'Golden Celebration'

Rosa
'Pink Grootendorst'

Rosa mundi

Rosa
'White Meidiland'

Rosa
'Mary Rose'

modern roses. Some are bushy and some even arch gracefully, while others are upright, best used as punctuations.

David recommended planting a single variety in groups of three. I had done this with the six 'Sea Foam' but hadn't taken the idea further. A grouping makes a better show sooner, with more heft, more blooms, and a longer bloom time as each shrub has slightly different timing. Following his advice, I place the holes in a triangle 18 inches apart so the plants grow together to form a single robust mass.

Pruning Roses

David also demystified pruning for me. His commonsense approach: Remove the dead or diseased stems as they appear, but don't cut out all the new thin stems. They will grow to produce a stronger, healthier bush. After a number of years, take out one or two of the older stems to encourage new main growth. And that's all.

Traditional pruning techniques vary with different roses. Hybrid teas are supposed to be pruned to within 6 or 8 inches of their lives, shrubs to 2 feet, and climbers to three canes. I don't know who decided this, nor do I understand why. I have always let my roses grow freely to see what they can do, believing that the larger the bush, the more flowers it will produce. The relatively few hybrid teas left over from our grand purge now stand 6 feet tall and 4 feet wide and bloom prolifically. For me, pruning is more about size and shape than health. Robert Dash, at his ever-changing Madoo Conservancy in East Hampton, New York, has a *Rosa glauca* the size and shape of a small dogwood. He only let one cane grow and fatten into a trunk.

Rosarians recommend painstakingly cutting each cane on a 45-degree angle, slanting downward, above a node or an outward-facing leaf bud to encourage the bud to grow. Spreading the canes and looking for the correct node before each cut used to take me a half-hour or more for each bush. If I had continued doing it that way, I probably would have given up roses entirely long ago.

Now I prune roses as I do other shrubs. Older plants are hacked back each winter with a hedge clipper to a nicely rounded bush, usually about 3 or 4 feet high. I let young plants grow as they will for the first few years. If they have room to grow and their shape is pleasing, they might not need to be pruned at all. It is obvious that dead branches need removing, but why healthy ones? Supposedly, fewer canes produce larger flowers. But what's the point of slightly larger flowers if the blooms are closer to the ground and harder to see? I'm not entering any contests anyway.

In late fall I cut any excessively long stems on shrub roses and wayward branches on climbers to prevent damage by winter storms. Most of my roses grow into full-bodied, dense bushes. If they are spindly growers, they are pulled up and tossed out after 3 years' probation.

Because I frequently cut roses for the house, the plants are spot-pruned regularly. I cut stems to whatever lengths I need for the bouquet. For years I've thought it was nonsense to have to cut back to a full leaf. So I was grateful when I recently read about a rose trial conducted at the Royal National Rose Society gardens in England. The trial discovered that the way a rosebush is deadheaded radically affects its performance. When the bloom is snapped off at the neck, rather than cut back to the first full leaf, the bush has 50 percent more bloom.

Foxtail lilies among the roses draw the eye up with their exclamation marks.

a garden vignette

I was once convinced that I couldn't grow foxtail lilies, hybrids of *Eremurus*. I'd planted the bare rootstocks among the roses 2 years in a row, and nothing grew. I gave up for a few years, then decided to try again when I saw them growing in a friend's garden. This time, by chance, I ordered from a different nursery. The octopus-like roots that arrived were three times as big as the ones I had planted previously. It wasn't me—it was the nursery! When they dug up the roots, they had apparently broken off the ends of the tentacles. This time, I dug holes 6 inches deep and 14 inches wide, poured in an inch of fine gravel to ensure that the root would not sit in water, then topped the gravel with compost and soil. I set the crown of the root carefully at 2 inches below ground level so there was no chance of it rotting. My foxtail lilies are now my pride and joy. They soar 8 feet, dwarfing all else in the rose garden, and their 3-foot spires bloom for several weeks. The large flower heads begin blooming from the bottom up with hundreds of tiny bell-shaped flowers, thus assuring they look good for an extended period. Sorry about the bragging, but once I tame a difficult plant, it is hard to restrain myself.

Alliums, leeks, lupines, and lamb's ears grow at the base of *Rosa* 'Carefree Wonder'. The boxwood hedge keeps them from wandering onto the lawn.

PICKING FAVORITES

My rose bed is fairly settled now, and most years nothing changes. One of the top performers is 'Mutabilis', a unique China rose with single flowers that are yellow in bud, change to pink once they open, and finally fade to crimson. All the different stages and colors of bloom on the shrub at the same time is a glorious sight. If forced to choose a favorite (I'd frankly have trouble settling on a top 10), I would probably choose 'Abraham Darby' as much for its rich fruity perfume as for its old-fashioned blooms. Each deeply cupped blossom is apricot washed with pink and yellow. 'Heritage' comes a close second with delicate shell pink, cup-shaped flowers that dispense a heady perfume—overtones of fruit, honey, and carnation on a myrrh background. 'Mary Rose', an old favorite, is the first English rose I planted. Its shocking rosy pink flowers brighten the garden as its honey-and-almond scent lifts the spirits. On the opposite side, another outrageous, heart-stopping pink semi-double, 'Carefree Wonder', has tousled, unkempt petals that curl in different directions.

ROSE COMPANIONS

The original plan was to leave bare soil in the bed between the roses. This is traditional, but we found it neither practical nor attractive. Bare soil requires weekly weeding and distracts from the flowers. Soilborne diseases have a field day when rain spatters mud everywhere. Shallow-rooted groundcovers, on the contrary, blanket the soil beautifully, preventing the spread of disease, keeping the ground warmer in fall and cooler in summer, and slowing evaporation. If truly shallowly rooted, groundcovers don't compete with the deeper roots of the roses.

So although the roses are the center of attention in this garden, it is the chorus line of other bloomers that helps their beauty shine. Old-fashioned **catmint** serves as a groundcover, knitting the garden together with its cloud of blue flowers and silvery foliage. Alliums, leeks, foxtail lilies, ornamental poppies, Oriental lilies, blue lupines, and clematis sprout through it.

I love **giant alliums** (*Allium giganteum*) blooming among the roses. Each flower stem soars up to 3½ feet, needs no staking, and blooms with a globe of star-shaped flowers up to 10 inches across. I've planted them for many years, although they are among the most expensive bulbs and they rarely return in my heavy soil. So I've added multitudes of the inexpensive old reliables (*A. aflatunense*) and substituted

I have always let my roses grow freely, believing that the larger the bush, the more flowers it will produce.

flowering leeks as an exclamation mark. These good old-fashioned vegetables are usually relegated to the vegetable garden to be pulled up for soup at the end of their first year, but if left to grow into their second year, they will flower and set seed. They are perfectly hardy. They send up stems 6 feet high with 4-inch globes of blossom. Sometimes they even send up a second blooming stem, a sideshoot known as a leek pearl, right after the first. Their seedheads are decorative for several months and are great for drying. Growing among the roses, leeks are seldom recognized for what they are.

I admit that I'm bewitched by roses and I aim to please them. I do please most of them, most of the time. But there's only so much you can do—or try to do. Either a rose is susceptible to disease, or it isn't. Either it is happily situated, or it isn't. Either it is well bred, or it isn't. Now, if a rose doesn't perform, I blame the rose. Rose descriptions are often marketing ploys, not truths. The majority of roses introduced each year will not be around 10 years hence, and for good reason. Even award-winning roses have failings—I've tossed many a California or Florida beauty out on the street. Trial and error is the only way to grow beautiful roses. I think of it as a $15 bet. The odds are better for success with one of the English roses or a rose with a history.

a garden vignette

With so many variables in gardening, it isn't always possible to be sure why a plant doesn't grow as expected, but it pays to be suspicious. Nurseries have been known to sell me a dud with underdeveloped roots, and it's not easy to spot this when transplanting (unless it's already potbound, which is another matter). Last year in spring, I planted two identical roses in containers to fatten them up. One grew robustly, the other didn't, although it bloomed and looked healthy. In fall, when I moved them into the garden, I discovered that one had stunted roots, half the size of the other. I don't know why. I assume it was a birth defect.

A bank of roses

Because there are always new roses I want to try, and they won't all fit into the rose garden, I began planting the bank overlooking the pool with more roses. The roses I put here have to be tough as nails because they don't get much care. The bank slopes steeply down to the pool, and the roses hold the bank in place. They're closely planted and pruned just enough so I can get between them each winter to comfort them with compost. To keep the compost from washing down the hill in the steepest parts, I placed a revetment made out of three boards nailed together in front of each plant. Except for when I'm cutting them for bouquets, the rosebushes are viewed only from a distance.

Because the bank is near the swimming pool, it is a carnival of colors—anything goes, without apology. Here I grow yellows—'Graham Thomas' and 'Golden Wings'—and scentless roses—'Scarlet Meidiland', 'Coral Meidiland', 'White Meidiland', and 'Alba Meidiland', which make up for their lack of fragrance with prolific blooms and no sign of disease. 'Scarlet Meidiland' blooms in sprays of small scarlet roses until well after first frost. Described as a small shrub in catalogs, my 10-year-old one stands more than 6 feet tall. That's the beauty of not pruning.

At one time, the disparate Rosa 'Veilchenblau' was fighting with everyone. As its dark magenta flowers streaked with white fade over its 3 weeks of bloom, they change from violet-blue to an unearthly lilac. I thought it should bloom alone. It certainly depressed the nearby pink roses. Most troubling was its juxtaposition with 'Coral Meidiland'. There was no rest for years until I finally transplanted the thornless, semidouble climber across the pool to intertwine its limbs with 'Golden Showers' and 'Golden Celebration'. Basking in their sunshine has given 'Veilchenblau' a lift.

Both 'Belinda', a semidouble, and 'Ballerina', a single, bloom in arched sprays of tiny pink flowers clustered together, resembling elaborately embroidered skirts. I often cut a stem for nature's ready-made bouquet.

Five 'Bonica' line one side of the fence and three 'Eden' line the other. 'Bonica' blooms are medium pink double flowers that are good for cutting. They are trouble-free shrubs, or rather they were until I pruned one within inches of its life one spring. It has never grown as strongly or produced as many flowers since. The others I cut back only by a third when they reach out too far over the fence. 'Eden' has deeply cupped flowers packed with 115 petals. The outer rows of petals open a pristine white, in high contrast to their bright pink centers. Visitors always stop to gush.

There are four once-bloomers adorning the hillside. At the top of the bank are two long-limbed, gangly roses—scarlet 'Geranium', the earliest rose to bloom, and 'American Pillar', the last. They both billow over the wall and add beauty to the formal garden as well as to the rose bank. The other ones include the strongly perfumed 'Mme. Hardy', a white centifolia with more than 200 petals swooning down to a green eye, and R. glauca, grown more for its deep purple foliage that ages to soft plum and its maroon hips that ripen to orange. R. glauca's pasty pink single flowers don't garner much attention in contrast to those of R. mundi, which once seen are never forgotten. The carmine pink broad streaks that flow randomly across the blush white petals are a beautiful accident of nature, a chance offspring of 'Apothecary's Rose'.

The tough rugosa roses are perfectly suited for the hillside. R. rugosa rubra has flamboyant, single, deep magenta blooms arriving all season and quickly joined by bright orange hips that continue to ripen as the flowers

fade. 'Pink Grootendorst', a hybrid rugosa, blooms profusely with small fringed buttons that resemble carnations and bloom in tight clusters.

The hillside of roses has understory plants as well—mostly perennial thugs that duke it out amongst themselves. I don't pay much attention to their battles. Artemisia was originally planted in the middle of the hillside for its silver foliage. Inexplicably, it ran downhill and resides at the bottom, where it won't tolerate any other perennials. Hollyhocks hold court at the top, where they can gaze over the wall into the perennial garden.

The bank of roses is a mix of shrub, climbing, and antique roses: 'Coral Meidiland', 'Scarlet Meidiland', and 'Bonica' flourish on the fence. In the background 'American Pillar', *Rosa glauca*, and 'Cadwell Pink' bloom exuberantly.

Evening primroses in yellow and pink hold the middle ground. Queen Anne's lace, the roadside menace, gracefully dances throughout in welcome contrast to the roses. Its carrot-shaped roots hold the soil, and I can pull them up at will. Mostly I love Queen Anne's lace for bouquets.

For more than 15 years the hillside has cared for itself—a survival of the fittest. In the early years I replaced roses that couldn't make it on their own. It's been years since I've had to do that. The variety assures there is bloom from May through November.

The Flagstone Courtyard

The walled area beside the carriage house was never intended as the cottage garden it has turned into. Dealing with it wasn't even a priority until the grass became permanently rutted and disfigured by the kids' bikes and

The first year the sunflowers grew from seeds dropped by the birds. After enjoying them that first summer, we planted them every year after.

other traffic in and out of the carpentry shop. It was then that we hit upon the idea of enlarging the existing gardens lining the walls and the sides of the buildings

and replacing the grass in the courtyard with flagstones—much more in keeping with the age and mood of the house. The beds are now 5 feet deep, except where they bulge out to 12 feet to encompass a dogwood in the center of the courtyard.

the spaces between the paving stones have turned out to be perfect pockets for low growers: herbs such as thyme, lavender, and oregano; bulbs such as daffodils, snowdrops, crocus, and alliums; and assorted perennials and annuals such as creeping phlox, dwarf hosta, portulaca, lobelia, and ageratum. Frankly, it is a hodgepodge. There are also plants in pots, which makes it easy to move the color around. Plants spilling over the paving stones soften the hard edges of the yard. Fragrance rises to greet us whenever we step on the thyme, and this suggested adding perfumed flowers: sweet peas, alyssum, pinks, and roses. The walls keep the wind from roaring through and also trap the heat, encouraging the ground to warm up sooner. Bulbs bloom earlier, and flower fragrances linger longer.

Rose climbers define the space, taking the eye up 10 to 20 feet above the ground to where the flowers bloom. They help to make the area appear larger than it really is. Roses also dress our cold, gray stucco walls, beautifying them even from a distance.

Sometimes roses surprise me, reminding me not to take their behavior for granted. Climbing rose 'Margo Koster', with salmon-colored clusters of globe-shaped blooms the size of 50-cent pieces, grows on the playhouse. Its blossoms hang on canes that fan out over the back stucco wall, then head straight up the lat-

OPPOSITE: The pockets between the stones are perfect for annuals such as alyssum and sunflowers and perennials such as the golden creeping Jenny. Assorted hostas weave a tapestry of green under the dogwood.

ticework to the tower behind. It was advertised as a compact grower, perfect for small gardens, and in fact, if pruned in the traditional way, it stays less than 3 feet. I made the mistake of planting tall perennials in front of it, blocking its view and shading its roots, but over 10 years (during which time I didn't prune it), it has crept gradually up the wall. Each year it looked better as it gained weight and stood taller. 'Margo Koster' is now over the back wall of the carriage house and well up the playhouse tower. This proves to me that if you believe in a plant, encourage it to do its best, and don't acknowledge its limitations, it can accomplish amazing things.

The carpentry shop, the back wall, and the garden shed are now all embellished with roses as well. And if roses could add so much beauty, I reasoned, why not try other perennial vines? So I added trumpet vine, clematis, and honeysuckle to the mix. The climbers add to the lushness of the garden, and it seems bigger with the flowers blooming on the roof of the garden house, the carpentry shop, and the stucco walls and sides of the house.

The dogwood in the center of the yard is surrounded with an assortment of flowering groundcovers. They are low-growing, in scale with the tree. A single

a garden vignette

One thing you can count on is that plants will self-seed in the strangest places. One year a giant sunflower surprised me by popping up between the stones in the center of the terrace. Despite the awkward spot, it skyrocketed to 7 feet! I so admired its tenacity that I placed a chair beside it as if it were a standing lamp, so that it would feel more at home. Actually, the roots of a giant sunflower do mimic a lamp base, fanning out to form a shallow circle several feet in diameter. This provides sufficiently firm footing for the plant to stay upright through winter. Although a sunflower hangs its head, it is still a triumph of natural engineering.

Shady bloomers such as pink double impatiens, white coneflowers, and hostas join the sun-loving iris to add color to the garden.

variety could have done the trick, but in this small space, it would have been monotonous, so I planted an assortment for continuous bloom—bergenia, epimedium, dwarf hosta, astilbe, and lirope. For summer color, I tuck in some double impatiens.

In the back corner of the courtyard, I have pruned a rose-of-Sharon 'Diana' high enough to make room for flowers underneath. Pruned like a tree, rose-of-Sharon becomes an altogether more desirable and beautiful plant than if allowed to remain shrubby. It is 9 feet high now, so in August and September I have flowers overhead. The white hibiscus flowers glow when hit by sunlight, and the blooms last a couple of months. A flowering tree is hard to come by in late summer while blooming shrubs are plentiful, so I ended up making pseudo-trees out of all the rose-of-Sharons on the property.

The courtyard garden consistently soldiers on with something interesting always happening. The tree peonies under the bay window bloom for only a few weeks, but the salad-plate–size flowers are an invariable topic of conversation with visitors. While they are blooming, the rest of the garden could be a desert and no one would notice. The blossoms open near the bottom of the plant first and are often hidden by the foliage above, so I always pick a few for the house. A single flower is an arrangement in itself.

After the perennials die back and the dogwood and the ivy lose their leaves, we are reminded of how small this courtyard space actually is. It grows in size again once the bergenia blooms and the first tiny snowdrops appear, and the foliage gradually softens and beautifies the harshness of the flagstones. It always amazes me how many different plants grow happily together here. There is almost always a flower coming into bloom.

The courtyard garden consistently soldiers

on with something interesting always happening.

High hopes

If a climbing red rose hadn't come with our carriage house when we bought it, I might not have fallen so hopelessly in love with climbers, nor would I have come to realize that more than one climber could flourish in the same space.

The previous owners left the walls of the building clothed in Boston ivy, plus one nameless climbing rose. By the time we moved in, the rose was already several decades old. It reached up and over the bay window, wrapping it in ribbons of bloom. The ivy served as its trellis, offering a place for the rose's thorns to catch as it pulled itself skyward. Tentatively, I added more climbers and over time realized how little care they require. The ivy supports the roses and also hides any battered rose foliage. Climbing roses, remember, don't really climb; at least not the way vines do. Most of them lean, sprawl, arch, and creep up or scramble over the ground, stretching out their awkward canes into anything available. Some climb 20 to 30 feet and beyond, while others grow only 8 to 12 feet.

I discovered if I planted the roses 3 feet away from a building, angling them so their canes point toward the wall instead of straight up into the air, they almost take care of themselves. When the young canes reach the house, they are flexible enough to curve upward,

Once-a-summer bloomer *Rosa* 'American Pillar' *(above)* blooms her heart out for a month on the carriage house joined by *Rosa* 'Dorothy Parker', a small pink double.

and their thorns tend to hook into the ivy. They begin the climb on their own. If they come free and wave to me, I gently tie them onto or weave them under the ivy to help them get a grip. At the beginning, I pruned out the dead or ornery canes that stuck out in the wrong direction until I realized it wasn't really necessary. The climbers now planted against the house can go where they want as long as they don't obstruct the chimney or cover a window. (And even so, there is something to be said for a rose grinning in at a window.)

With the shorter climbers, I gently arch each cane into a fan shape against the wall, loosely securing it. Horizontal branches are the secret to full, all-out bloom. With branches arched into a more horizontal position, more of the cane is exposed to the sun, and more shoots develop along it, encouraging more flowers to form at each node.

In July an 'American Pillar' rose shimmies up the chimney and sends a cane or two around the corner to enliven two sides of the house at once. In order to add yet another rose at the side of the building, where cement prevented any planting, I built a wooden box 3 feet deep and filled it with topsoil and compost. It will be another 2 years before I know whether this arrangement will work, but I am hopeful.

The Lilac and Peony Walk

Designing and building a garden can be a daunting task unless it is broken down into manageable steps. I usually start with a pair of plants, then build a community of plants around them. Sometimes it's as simple as repeating

On the outside of the walk, the dark foliage of the smoke bush contrasts with late-blooming Chinese lilacs.

145

clumps of the same plants at intervals throughout the garden. I didn't realize it at first, but it is impossible for me to restrict a garden to two plants, even if planted en masse.

What started as a lilac and peony walk became a fragrant path with scented blooms most of the year. All that is missing now, in fact, is winter bloom—and it isn't needed because the walk is rarely frequented in winter. (But then again, if I tucked in a few witch hazels, that would change . . . perhaps I will.)

this S-shaped path stretches between the formal flower garden and the kitchen garden, softly curving twice en route. Pink lilacs darken to blue and purple in the middle, where pink and red peonies form a climax. White lilacs surrounded by white peonies mark each end of the walk.

The path, as designed, originally featured 18 lilacs planted in three clusters of six, spaced equally. Each group of six was divided, with three on each side of the path. The original group was selected to provide the full range of doubles and singles planted in colors moving from white to soft pinks to blues and purples before fading back to white. Most were cultivars of the common lilac (*Syringa vulgaris*), the strongest-scented species of lilacs and the longest blooming (typically from 16 to 20 days). All have the true lilac scent, the one most prized.

We mixed several later-blooming Chinese lilacs (*S. villosa*) in the pink section to extend the bloom. Their lavender pink flowers come at the same time as the mid- and late-blooming peonies in early June. *S. villosa* doesn't

An assortment of early- to mid-blooming peonies flower with late-blooming lilacs to turn the walk into a perfumed passageway.

have the true lilac scent but rather a pleasing musky perfume with spicy undercurrents. At the head of the path, peeking over the formal garden wall, we placed a pink-flowered tree form of the littleleaf lilac (*S. pubescens* subsp. *microphylla*). It exhales a light musk and is the last to bloom, thus letting us down slowly.

Clumps of **peonies** surround each group of lilacs. 'Festiva Maxima', dating back to 1851, was already in the garden when we bought the house. (I identify with such "old lady" peonies. Their longevity proves they were valued.) It has large bowls of double white flowers that are uniquely splashed in the center with flecks of red, making the cultivar easy to identify. It is the first peony along the walk to bloom, usually as the common lilacs are finishing, and its scent is reminiscent of sweet talcum powder. 'Festiva Maxima' joins white lilacs at the entrance to the kitchen garden and is a counterpart to 'Baroness Schröder', planted near the white lilacs at the other end, at the entrance to the formal flower garden. 'Baroness Schröder', born in 1889, has rose-shaped, double white flowers faintly tinged with pink and is a late bloomer. Late-blooming peonies are not plentiful, and the peony season is short, so I cherish the ones I find.

When peonies bloom their hearts out, they lack the strength and backbone to hold their heads up. I am very supportive, girdling each with a green peony ring. Once their foliage grows up and through the rings, the rings are invisible.

Searching for ways to extend the scent and beauty of the lilac and peony walk, I decided to plant three tree peonies. Tree peonies differ from the typical herbaceous ones in that their woody stems don't die back to the ground in winter; they grow almost as wide as tall, ultimately reaching 4 feet. Their extra-large flowers, often the size of salad plates, are a marvel of engineering. The petals may be crinkled like crepe paper or silken and translucent with the look of fine porcelain. I excuse picking many of them just as they open by claiming to spare them the battering of spring wind and rain. Usually, the first blooms that open are hidden by foliage near the bottom of the bush, so they don't make much of a showing in the

BELOW: The flowers of a tree peony like this pink one can be the size of a salad plate. OPPOSITE: The common lilac (*Syringa vulgaris*) is the most strongly scented and typically blooms before the peonies.

Late-blooming peonies are not plentiful, so I cherish the ones I find.

garden anyway. In any event, the flowers last longer and their breathtaking beauty can be admired better indoors, away from harm.

I placed the tree peonies 'Guardian of the Monastery', 'Hephestos', and an unnamed yellow midway in the walk to bloom before the lilacs. They often stay on to greet the trusses of lilac bloom and blend their sweet scents. 'Guardian of the Monastery' has huge blooms, averaging 10 inches across. The semidouble layers of crinkled petals are cream with wide swaths of lavender melting into raspberry flares running down the middle of each petal, all radiating out from a golden mound of stamens. 'Hephestos' is the only double tree peony I grow, and its flowers are slightly smaller than 'Guardian of the Monastery'. It is a deep ruby red with pointed and

A view of the lilac and peony path in the early years before it expanded from 18 to 29 lilacs and to three times as many peonies.

ruffled petals. The nameless yellow is not as showy as the other two, with single flowers close to 6 inches across, but it is more prolific, and its smaller blooms are not as fragile. For the most part, I leave these on the bush to be enjoyed in the garden.

Scented Companions

The path struck me as a little bare early in the season, before the lilacs leafed out or the peonies showed their faces. So I planted clusters of daffodils and Siberian squill under the bare branches of shrubs. The bulbs have naturalized there and refuse to be crowded out by the lilacs' increasing spread. A strip of grass between the brick path and the lilac bed became a problem to mow, so out it came and was replaced by **St. John's-wort**. This blooms in midsummer and sporadically into late fall. The green leaves turn reddish brown after a prolonged cold spell but cling to the stems until I give them a haircut in late winter, just before the new growth starts. The original narrow strip of St. John's-wort has now crept back between the peonies and scooted under the lilacs to knit the path together. The peonies are not bothered by St. John's-wort breathing down their necks.

On the sunny southern side of the path, we planted a **southern magnolia** (*Magnolia grandiflora*) to add a vertical accent to one curve in the path and to blast a loud and heady sweet scent in the hot and humid days of summer. A couple of **daphne** nearby also help to extend the bloom season. Lilac daphne (*Daphne genkwa*) blooms in a frightful shade of purple, sometimes in March, most often in April. But because nothing else in the vicinity is in bloom at the time, it can't get into a fight. Caucasian daphne (*D. caucasica*) starts to bloom in April and doesn't stop until November or December. It is strongly scented. I don't know a more giving shrub.

Back 10 feet from the path, on the same side as the magnolia, a tall **yellowwood** (*Cladrastis lutea*) blooms in May, spreading its fragrance—a pronounced vanilla scent with deep notes of hyacinth—from its pendulous ropes of white pealike flowers. Then the rambling rose 'Seagull' climbing the yellowwood's trunk takes over. Rose blossoms tumble down from the bottom branches of the tree for 3 weeks in June after the lilacs and peonies have finished. I bottom-pruned the rose to three stems, training them to follow the trunk to the first limb; from there they found their own path, climbing branches to seek the sun. When I wasn't looking, the rose added more canes, but I've let them be as long as they grow upward and don't reach out and grab passersby.

The back of the north side of the path is shaded by the pin oaks that line the driveway. The trees are limbed up, however, so there is a fair amount of indirect light and a few hours of direct sun that passes under their branches. Here I added first one, then two, then three **smoke bushes** (*Cotinus coggygria*). It took me a while to realize that their purple foliage was the perfect foil for the green of the lilacs. The dark foliage marks the back of the path, separating it from the brambles behind that hide the driveway and shelter the birds.

Looking for more scented plants and even more dark foliage, I hit upon *Rosa glauca* and *R. 'Mme. Hardy'*.

The once-blooming rose 'Seagull' climbs the yellowwood's trunk and garlands its branches with clusters of white scented roses in June, just after the tree has finished flowering.

Both bloom only once, early in the season. The Pepto-Bismol pink flowers of *R. glauca* are not much to look at, as garden writer Anne Raver notes, but its dark foliage and ornamental hips are fabulous. When grown in full sun, the rose produces new growth that is a deep purple, which ages to soft plum washed with silver. Two of these joined the crowd at the back. Here, in shade, the foliage is slightly paler with a grayish cast. It is attractive all season in the garden and in flower arrangements,

What started as a lilac and peony walk became a fragrant path with scented blooms most of the year.

where it combines beautifully with pink and rosy flowers. The hips begin as deep maroon and ripen to orange. Starting in midsummer, hips of both colors dangle together in sharp contrast to the dark foliage.

Pushing the limits, I planted 'Mme. Hardy' on the theory that as an early bloomer, it might form its buds and begin to bloom before the overhead trees leaf out. This has worked well. One of the finest and purest white roses, 'Madame Hardy' has flowers that glow against its dark green foliage, with a strong, sweet fragrance that

The first peonies begin to bloom with the later-blooming lilacs (*Syringa villosa*).

has just a hint of lemon. Introduced as a cross between a damask and an alba or a centifolia, the quartered flowers open cupped but flatten out on top as the outer petals reflex, curving downward to reveal green button-eye centers (or pips). Occasionally, hints of a pink blush appear on some flowers. It blooms only once a season but for more than a month. I haven't pruned it. I'm encouraging it to grow as big as the lilacs.

As I've discovered other lilacs and peonies, I've deepened the borders, gradually expanding the collection until there are now 29 lilacs and three times as many peonies. It was a simple idea that took on a life of its own. After all, if you have to go from here to there, down a fragrant path is the most delightful way to walk.

A time of drought

The summer of 2002 was one to forget. The garden was defeated early on by the worst drought and highest heat recorded in decades. Fall wasn't much better. It sizzled out without a flame. My struggles against this double whammy of record-breaking heat and drought drained me, too.

The garden wore its scars on its singed, scorched, and parched foliage and had little energy left for the flowers and fruit. The lawn, perhaps the smartest, retreated into a coma of brown straw but later recovered.

Our deep well gurgled and grunted often during that summer, so we had to give it a rest. Playing Gunga Din (not too successfully, I might add) to plants beyond the reach of the sprinkler was my summer workout. None of the usual midsummer garden activities took place: no moving of plants from one area to another, no new plants added from nursery excursions, no seeds started for next year's perennials. Even weeding was a nonevent. The garden went on hold, awaiting relief from the heavens.

Was Mother Nature telling us something about the value of water that we didn't already appreciate? My garden confirmed many things I already knew. The plants most hurt were the water guzzlers. Hydrangea flowers, after hanging their heads frequently throughout summer, browned long before their time. Even with irrigation, flowers and fruits were noticeably smaller. Roses and tomatoes were the worst hit. The rose blossoms were less plentiful and smaller than usual. So were the tomatoes. As if that wasn't bad enough, excessive heat hurried the annuals out of bloom, and perennials bloomed for shorter periods of time. Even tough roadside wild-

Zinnias make perfect landing pads for butterflies.

flowers—Joe-pye weed, ironweed, black-eyed Susan—that looked un-scathed were more dwarf than usual.

But there were happy surprises as well. Many plants took drought in their stride, and the contrast between them and the tenderfeet made me sit up and take notice. Hostas with their large broad leaves fared well, while their shady neighbors, the astilbes, browned and entered dormancy early. Some astilbes failed to return the following year. Zinnias—Mexicans at heart—like it hot and dry. Clethra never looked so good nor bloomed so much. And in dry soil, the slugs were nowhere to be seen. Herbs looked no worse for the wear, and some—particularly basil and lavender—thrived. It was apparent that artemisia, lamb's ear, and sedum—plants with silvery, hairy, or fleshy foliage that slows water loss through transpiration—experienced no difficulty in handling the drought.

Drought has a telescoping effect on the seasons, and fall was upon us sooner than usual. Now I was discouraged. Everywhere I looked, trouble stared me in the face—browned leaves, a half-dead tree, decimated primroses, leafless roses, dwarfed annuals.

What saved me from despair was recognizing the opportunity for reassessment and redesign, to see what worked and what didn't. I realized that I'd been putting off dealing with those parts of the gardens that I disliked because the plants there were healthy. Now they weren't.

Once I dug in and began making changes, I felt better. As my creative juices flowed, my adrenaline did, too. Mother Nature had given me the kick in the pants I needed. The year 2002 was not one to forget, after all.

The Shrinking Lawn

I've never understood the cult of the lawn and the lengths people go to keep lawns green. One reason is that I'm against polluting the earth with chemical fertilizers and weed killers, but another reason is that lawns strike me as

Two fringe trees at the end of a clump of witch hazels bloom in late June in an island in the lawn, then fruit in fall with clusters of blue berries.

monotonous and boring. It's shouldn't be hard for you to imagine what my lawn looks like. Ken Druse, a highly respected garden writer, drolly suggested that mine was a closely chopped meadow.

Our neighbors on both sides take the opposite position. Their houses each sit high on a hill and have sweeping lawns that run down to the bay, an open invitation for flocks of geese to swoop in and take charge. The squishy plops the geese leave behind require some high stepping to reach the beach. Thankfully, the geese don't like it at our house. They never visit. The trees and shrubs on our bank frame our view and discourage them from flying in. I've freely given both neighbors advice about planting more trees, a hedge, or an island of shrubs, but to no avail. Their solution was to buy noisy cannons that shoot blanks and to blast off a round whenever the geese touch down. It's quite something then to watch the geese take flight, circle around for 10 minutes, and land again right on the original spot. At times, when both neighbors have their artillery going at the same time, I feel as though I'm in a war zone. I can only hope they'll soon tire of the game.

If it weren't for the family pastimes of croquet, badminton, and soccer, I'd do away with even more of our lawn than I already have. As it is, I've invited bulbs and wildflowers in. In early spring, snowdrops, crocuses, and scillas bloom in the lawn, followed by dandelions that complement the *(continued on page 160)*

OPPOSITE: An ornamental crab-apple tree and a linden are dressed with skirts of early blooms, including tulips and forget-me-nots.

I decided that a tree isn't fully dressed

without a flowering petticoat.

daffodils in the meadow. I enjoy the dandelions; like the roses, they put on a major show in spring and bloom sporadically all summer and fall.

For some reason, gardeners usually cherish the kind of blue offered by **creeping penstemon** (*Veronica repens*) but disdain this little creeper. I love its blue puddles scattered across the lawn. At one time—briefly, though, because it didn't add much—I let it creep into the flower borders.

Clover, especially the four-leaf ones, brings us more than luck: In bloom, it's snow-on-the-grass of summer. The only reason I remove it from the places we walk is to protect the bees. In summer a member of my barefoot family always steps on one.

Dressing the Trees

My practice of carving out chunks of lawn to plant flowers began in self-defense. I could not bear to have the crab apple tree on the front lawn banged, bruised, and beaten by the lawn mower one more time. So I surrounded the trunk with a defensive circle of silver-toned, furry lamb's-ear. Suddenly, the other trees looked naked. I decided that a tree isn't fully dressed without a flowering petticoat.

Ever since, I've been whittling away at the lawn, replacing large chunks around the bases of trees with strategically placed groundcovers—sometimes to solve a problem, sometimes just because it looks better that way. I choose low-growing shrubs, herbs, or perennials that spread over the ground, bloom, and suppress weeds. Wood chips might do the same, but they are nowhere nearly as attractive. I have to admit that groundcovers require a certain amount of work; despite the advertisements, there is no such thing as a no-maintenance solution. The plants need their soil replenished yearly with compost and occasional weeding. So for just a little more work, I have more flowers.

As for size, I make the tree's petticoat at least equal to the spread of its canopy. If the tree is fast-growing, I make the circle one-third larger—but never smaller. Smaller looks skimpy. Under an ornamental tree, I may choose a groundcover to bloom with the tree for a better show. Smaller trees can be nicely dressed with a single plant repeated around its trunk. A larger tree can handle clusters of different plants weaving together into a more creative garden. No great degree of invention is required. Even the "Big Three"—**pachysandra, periwinkle,** and **ivy**—can be attractive when lavishly embroidered with an underplanting of bulbs such as daffodils, snowflakes, wood hyacinth, or colchicum.

Between my car's refusal to drive past a nursery without a quick look-see and my habit of perusing every catalog in my mailbox, I have discovered many interesting named varieties of those three old standbys. On *Pachysandra terminalis* 'Silver Edge', each spoon-shaped leaf is rimmed in white, giving a subtle dappled effect. **Periwinkle** has both a white-edged variety, *Vinca minor* 'Sterling Silver', and a yellow one called 'Aureola'. Come spring, each is spangled with powder blue flowers. Other periwinkles have solid green leaves and delicate blooms: 'Miss Jekyll' sports a dainty white flower while 'Atropurpurea' is a knockout in plum. I've planted them all.

English ivies, which are evergreen all winter, come in more than 60 varieties with leaves of many sizes and in shapes resembling fans, diamonds, bird's feet, and hearts. 'Glacier' is splashed with white and has made itself at home in our woodland garden. 'Gold Heart' holds a pot of gold in the center of its heart-shaped leaf; recently, I planted it to climb the trunk of an ornamental cherry. The original 'Gold Heart' decorates the carpentry shop. Its offspring cover the entrance pillars and now the cherry tree. The gold glitters, winking at us across the lawn all year, but I am more aware of it in winter when its stems turn red. I underplanted the ivy with spring bulbs and filled in gaps with yellow petunias. Both ivies readily grow from cuttings.

'Gold Heart' ivy lights up a shady spot in summer and adds substance and color in winter when its evergreen leaves deepen in color and the stems blush red.

I attempted a more elaborate spring garden surrounding a young linden tree. Within the tree canopy, I planted daffodils, crocuses, and scillas, which anticipated the blossoms of tulips and peonies that were planted just *outside* of the canopy. After the peonies flowered, their foliage stayed on to ring the tree all summer, putting on a colorful display in tones of honey in fall. The arrangement worked fine for 5 years. But then the fast-growing tree broadened to the point where it shaded out the peonies. It was predictable; I had put the cart before the horse. The solution was to move the peonies to circle a Korean mountain ash, a slim-growing tree, which will not shade them. They may now stay there for decades.

Around another linden, I planted early spring-blooming bulbs followed by forget-me-nots. As the forget-me-nots die back, assorted hostas and daylilies poke through on the outskirts of the tree's leafy canopy. Most of the other trees on the lawn got simple skirts of a single species. A crab apple blooms atop flounces of

lily-of-the-valley. A purple beech and an ornamental cherry have been livened up with a hoop skirt of St. John's-wort.

St. John's-wort is my old dependable, the perfect companion. I rely on him often. He never complains the soil is too heavy, doesn't care if it's sunny or shady, and is not invasive. Like hostas, St. John's-wort can be divided yearly and is most cooperative when sent to the far reaches of the property to start a new colony.

Islands of Bloom

after dressing the trees, I dug up island beds for shrubs. At a curve in the driveway, we started with six 'Arnold Promise' witch hazels to brighten our comings and goings in winter. Actually, witch hazel has two seasons of interest—in November, when its leaves color like the plumage on an exotic bird, deep orange feathering to yellow at the tips, and in midwinter, when it flowers.

a garden vignette

Confusingly, colchicum is commonly called autumn crocus. Colchicums (*Colchicum*) and autumn-flowering crocuses (*Crocus speciosus*) do look similar, and both bloom in fall, but up close they are very different. Colchicum flowers and bulbs are generally larger with six stamens in the centers of the blooms. Crocuses have only three stamens. The flowering stems of colchicum are naked of any leaves, while multiple blooms, 6 to 12 per corm, open one after another. In spring the leaves shoot up 15 inches like daffodil foliage on steroids. They are lush and green for a time before they turn a ghastly shade of yellow, appearing to be in agony, and die a slow death. Still, I assure you, the flowers are worth the weeks of misery. Do as I do, and look the other way as you walk by.

FROM OPPOSITE, LEFT, TO ABOVE, RIGHT: In April, early daffs and forget-me-nots bloom under the 'Arnold Promise' witch hazel. In September, fall crocus and colchicum bloom at their feet. In November, the witch hazel leaves turn fiery yellow and red before they fall. In midwinter, they bloom even under snow.

To extend the witch hazel's bloom, we underplanted a mix of early-, mid-, and late-blooming daffodils that start as the witch hazel is finishing. In June two fringe trees, one male and one female, bloom alongside the witch hazel. Grown in full sun or moderate shade, the **American fringe tree** (*Chionanthus virginicus*) can ultimately be a wide-spreading shrub or a small tree, reaching 20 feet at maturity. Its late-spring flowers bloom in fleecy white cascades, each branch extravagantly trimmed with fringelike blossoms. They sparkle against the green foliage and can be seen and enjoyed from anywhere along the driveway. Here again nature has favored the males with longer petals, up to 1¼ inches. Strangely, according to Michael Dirr, America's leading expert on woody plants, there appears to be a correlation between leaf width and petal width—the wider the leaf, the wider the petal. (Now that's a good shopping tip.) The sweet scent is subtle, yet on a warm, still day, it's still perceptible from several yards away.

In summer the fringe trees are quiet, simply dressed in green, but in fall the female tree bears navy blue fruit, hanging in clusters like grapes. It is worth the effort to plant a male and a female to get the fruit; it is beautiful dangling against the bright yellow fall foliage, as long as it's not too quickly consumed by the birds. No wonder the fringe tree was a favorite of Thomas Jefferson, who grew it at Monticello.

Under the flowering crab apple (*Malus* 'Donald Wyman'), forget-me-nots, daffodils, and ajuga live and bloom together.

Elsewhere on the shrinking lawn, we planted **leadwort** (*Plumbago*), which wove its way between and around the shrubs to produce bloom in late summer and long into fall. After that, it departs in a blaze of glorious bronze red foliage. An assortment of colchicum cultivars rise through the blue leadwort in September into October, putting on quite a show. What an improvement over wood-chip mulch!

Combining three different cultivars of **colchicums** extends the bloom in the bed. 'Lilac Wonder' is the most prolific bloomer with smaller vase-shaped, rosy purple flowers. 'The Giant' has larger goblets of lilac-pink flowers, and 'Waterlily' resembles its name, blooming last with large, double, rosy lilac flowers. The flowers are so heavy that they lay their heads down when it rains and raise them up again when the sun dries them off.

Colchicum bulbs are expensive, several dollars for a single one. I don't quite understand this because they naturalize and multiply so readily. The McClure & Zimmerman Quality Flowerbulb catalog and planting guide states that, "Ants relish the seed coating of colchicum . . . thereby spreading intact embryos to naturalize areas with fall blooms." Every few years I dig up some as their foliage is dying back, remove the baby corms from the mother, and replant them in another place. They are remarkably self-sufficient little creatures. The first fall I bought them, I was surprised to open the box and find a corm in bloom. Carrying their own food supply, which is replenished each spring before the foliage dies back, they can flower indoors without water or soil. If planted outdoors immediately after blooming, they regain their strength and carry on as if nothing happened.

To make the entrance to the house more welcoming, we planted a bed in the shape of a bow tie in the grass across from the front door where the driveway circles around. I can guess what you are thinking. But the shape has fortunately been obliterated as the shrubs bulged out over the years. At first the bow tie was dotted with spring bulbs, followed by a swirl of annuals. It was labor intensive to replant each year, however, so over time it evolved into a shrub border with four shrub roses at the back, a pair of vitex flanking each side, and an ornamental dogwood in the middle. The greater height is an improvement. It hides and distracts from the driveway. A decorative birdbath went in among the shrubs. The spring bulbs still bloom on the edges of the garden and between the shrubs. On the whole, the planting now takes little care beyond the usual scoops of compost, occasional haircuts, and twice-yearly weeding.

So much for lawns. My own opinion is that America could be transformed and beautified overnight if we could convince home owners riding their mowers to yield a little space for flowers. With less to mow, they'd make up the labor expended in one summer.

a garden vignette

The Korean mountain ash (*Sorbus alnifolia*) deserves to be better known. It alternates heavy bloom one year with light bloom the next. In May the tiny white flowers appear, held in flat-topped clusters of 6 to 10, similar to those of a viburnum. But I didn't plant the tree for its flowers. It's the berries I wanted. Several years ago, I was touring Hofstra Arboretum on the back of a golf cart with Jim Cross, Long Island's most respected grower, when he bolted out of the cart to inspect a tree. The bright rosy pink berries covering the mountain ash couldn't be missed. Neither of us had seen the tree before. Jim added it to his ever-expanding list of new plants, and I was lucky to receive one before his untimely death. This is a perfect example of an undermarketed tree. Michael Dirr called it "spectacular, at its best perhaps the handsomest of all mountain ash for fruit effect." With this kind of praise, it may become easier to find. I hope so.

A little help from the birds

In the garden, the birds sing and amuse us with their shenanigans. Trying to identify which particular kind is doing the singing is like learning a foreign language. Robins always wish us well; their typical greeting, "cheerily, cheerio, cheeriup, cheerily," puts any day in the garden into the right context. I'm thrilled when I recognize certain songs—the cardinals' "purdy, purdy, purdy—whoit, whoit, whoit," the raucous calls of the blue jays, the nasal notes of the nuthatch, along with the more obvious cries of crows, woodpeckers, and morning doves. I'm breaking the code.

Over the years, as we added more and more gardens, the number of birds that call our property home has increased dramatically. From a bird's point of view, an inviting garden includes a place to hide, as well as sources of water and food. We left wild corners and corridors on the outskirts of our land and a thicket of forsythia and multiflora roses along the driveway under the pin oaks as shelters. The ponds and many birdbaths provide plenty of water. A diversity of insects and plants bearing berries, nuts, and seeds keep them well fed.

The birds know that I don't use poisons. During their early spring migrations, huge flocks of different species land on our front lawn. I'll never forget the Sunday yellow warblers paid us a visit on their spring migration tour. Every tree sparkled as if hung with golden nuggets. When they flocked on the ground, you would have thought the sun had fallen and shattered, its rays gleaming in all directions. The next day, the warblers' landing in Central Park made the front page of the *New York Times.*

Every bird in a flock that lands pokes in the lawn and the driveway, dining on grubs and worms and heaven knows what else; then the flock moves gradually over every bit of open land. They are my secret weapon in bug warfare. It's clear that their sheer numbers keep the insect population at bay.

I am especially grateful that the birds eat so many grubs. Lumping them all together, "white grubs" are the single most damaging insect pest on lawns. Grubs of different species of beetles are similar—$\frac{1}{2}$ inch to 1 inch long, white to gray coloration, tan to brown head, and three pairs of legs. Whenever I uncover them, they squirm into a fetal position, curved like the letter C. They know they are about to be pinched. Even with a magnifying glass, it is difficult to tell grubs apart. One of the most damaging is the Japanese beetle. In summer the mated females lay approximately 60 eggs in moist soil, 3 inches deep. The larvae hatch into grubs that eat the roots of grass and plants for months before hibernating for winter. The next summer they emerge as beetles to attack the fruit and flowers. Thanks to the birds, Japanese beetle sightings are rare in our garden, though common in our neighbors' gardens.

We've had many wonderful sightings of birds over the years. An osprey arrived one day carrying a large fish and alighted atop a dead tree, staying all afternoon. The kids called friends to watch. A red-tailed hawk let us get a closer look when he napped on the balcony off the second-floor landing. More than once, we have sighted great blue herons fishing for goldfish in our pond. It was such a small pond for such a big bird that the proportions seemed all out of whack. Standing on one foot, his S-shaped neck cocked, a heron can shoot forward with incredible speed and spear the fish with his bill. I value the fish, but what a show!

The house finches used to return to nest in our hanging baskets each spring. They are not fussy guests, feeling equally at home regardless of what I plant—ivy geraniums, fuchsia, begonias, or impatiens. I once had my doubts about letting them stay there. The basket obviously needed to be watered, and I tried to decide between sacrificing the plants and attempting to move the nest. Neither alternative seemed satisfactory. So when the time came, I simply watered as gently and carefully as I could, avoiding the nest. The mother finch flew away when I approached but resumed her post when I left, and from then on we coexisted.

A bird nested and raised her family among the thorny canes of the rose 'Aloha'.

In subsequent years, finches built at least one and sometimes as many as four nests in different hanging baskets around the porch. The plants grew beautifully lush, probably because of baby bird droppings (we never saw droppings on the porch).

Because the baskets were so full of plants, visitors didn't notice the nests unless I pointed them out. One day, however, my daughter Catie brought home an alley cat and begged to keep it. The cat had no trouble finding the nests. To this day, I don't understand how he jumped straight up 7 feet to reach them, but he did. I was in the house when the racket erupted on the porch. When I arrived, the cat was sitting quietly licking his paws. The finch was clearly upset, hopping from chair to chair, screeching and dive-bombing at the cat. I sympathized with the bird. But the bird, I'm happy to say, learned his lesson and passed the message along. It has been years since finches nested in the hanging

baskets. I only hope they'll return in a decade or so, when the cat is gone.

Only finches liked the hanging baskets, but other birds have nested in the trees, in the ivy on the house, and among the climbing roses. I counted six nests last winter on the front of the house alone. Two bird's nests shared our climbing rose over the back door, one was in the climbing rose over the kitchen garden seat, and another in the arbor at the entrance to the orchard. Curiously, one bird chose to nest in the middle of a shrub rose too close to the ground in the formal garden. No sooner had the babies hatched than they were snatched. Over last winter I found two more nests in shrub roses by the front door. They were so well hidden that I'd missed them in spring.

Before visitors arrive, I usually drop a flower or two into each birdbath to add a little color. Mysteriously, a few hours later or the next morning, the flowers are on the ground. I solved the mystery one hot and humid afternoon while lazily sprawled in the hammock. (The educational opportunities offered by a hammock never cease to amaze me.) A robin deliberately picked up the flowers and threw them out, then proceeded to take his bath. Was the flower invading his territory? Didn't he appreciate beauty? Now I make a point of putting flowers in the birdbaths simply to see how long they'll stay there. It is a game the birds and I play.

Gardening Up

Somewhere along the way in my never-ending quest for more flowers, I realized the only place left to garden was up. Since I fell head over heels for vines, they have lent their charm to everything from shrubs, trees, and woody vines to stumps, masonry

In late May, two once-blooming roses, the petite-flowering 'Cecile Brunner' and the large-flowered 'Mme. Grégoire Staechelin', lock arms to put on a glorious show on the children's playhouse.

walls, doorways, porches, and chimneys to decorative trellises, gazebos, and arbors. I'm convinced that everything looks better cloaked in green.

t he vines I've used include annual cup-and-saucer vine, morning glories and moonflowers, perennial wisteria, honeysuckle, trumpet vine, assorted clematis, silver lace vine, cross vine, and climbing hydrangea. In addition to the vines, over the last 15 years I have added four or five dozen climbing roses of approximately two dozen different varieties that are repeated around the yard.

Most climbers do not resent a close neighbor and take up only a square foot or two of ground for their roots. They have developed survival techniques scrambling over more stationary plants and up all kinds of obstacles in their quest for the sun. These natural athletes scamper down hills, leap over streams, dangle from cliffs, shimmy up trees, walls, and fences, and do somersaults back down, twisting and turning gracefully as they go. Vines are more touched by wonder, endowed with beauty, and steeped in mystery than any other plants. Why do hops twine only clockwise and morning glories counterclockwise? Most vines have adapted to circle either way. Deadly nightshade (*Solanum dulcamara*) is a feeble twiner that goes in both directions. The great Charles Darwin was so fascinated by the subject that in the 1880s, he wrote *The Movements and Habits of Climbing Plants*. In the book he divides climbers into four groups: those that twine around a support, those that have the ability to clasp any object they touch, those that ascend by hooks, and those that climb with rootlets. While confined to his bed by illness, he patiently recorded how twining climbers growing in pots in his bedroom sweep in a circular motion in search of something to

OPPOSITE: Clematis 'Vyvyan Pennell' blooms in late spring with double flowers as it climbs *Rosa* 'Bonica'. In fall, it blooms again only with large single flowers.

On the wall at the entrance to our property, variegated ivy, cross vine, golden hops, and roses entwine, lushly embroidering the cement with flowers.

climb onto. On hops, for example, the first joints remain stationary. The "next one while very young may be seen to bend to one side and to travel slowly around toward all points of a compass, moving like the hands of a watch, with the sun." If a shoot is wound around a stick and the stick is withdrawn within a short time, the twiner retains its spiral for a time before straightening out and starting the process all over again. If the twiner has been spiraled around a support for a considerable amount of time, it will retain its spiral shape after the stick has been removed. Amazing!

All too many gardeners steer clear of climbers, not knowing, I suspect, how to take care of them. They certainly appear to need a great deal of attention, but in fact, most don't. Aside from welcoming occasional pruning and a bucket of compost to replenish their soil each year, they are self-reliant.

Climbers display a range of different behaviors. Simply put, there are drapers, clingers, grabbers, floppers, gropers, and tumblers. Some are loose-stemmed and happy-go-lucky; others are stiff and difficult. There are climbers to tame, climbers to tend, and climbers—fortunately, in the majority—that fend for themselves. Over the years I've learned the differences. Stronger climbers with stiff canes, such as climbing roses, and established clingers, such as Boston ivy, can act as a trellis for their other, more delicate brethren.

Annual Vines

In my timid days, I planted a lot of annual vines. They demand a minimal investment of money, but many require a nurturing hand, tucking them in and tying them up, until they are well on their way. For example, there is the cup-and-saucer vine (*Cobaea scandens*). Glimpsing it transported me down the rabbit hole to the Mad Hatter's tea party. The flowers resemble upside-down teacups hanging on the vine. The 2½-inch cups open pale green and magically turn lilac, then deepen to purple with white pinstripes. The flowers bloom at the end of sideshoots, making them easy to cut without disturbing the vine, and both the flowers and the seedheads are decorative for indoor bouquets.

Once started, cup-and-saucer vine climbs easily without much help, using foot-long corkscrew tendrils hooked at the end to do the job. Pull on the tendril for the fun of it, and it springs back. In frost-free climates, where it is perennial, the cup-and-saucer vine reaches 40 feet. In my garden, where it is an annual, it twines around a support and grows from 15 to 25 feet. It will take 4 months to bloom but then continues until hit by a prolonged frost. I have grown it up the Boston ivy that covers the posts on the back porch, up the bare legs of the climbing rose that hangs off the carriage house balcony, and on different arbors in the kitchen garden.

Vines are more touched by wonder, endowed with beauty, and steeped in mystery than any other plants.

Morning glories and moonflowers (both *Ipomoea*) are vines to twine together. Like an old married couple, they are compatible—one works days, the other nights. Morning glories open with the sun and close at twilight. Moonflowers open as the afternoon wanes to light up the night with dazzling white, 6-inch moons glowing against a backdrop of dark green foliage. The moonflower blooms last until midmorning of the following day. For a few glorious hours, the two vines party together.

Morning glories come in a host of other colors—scarlet, pale pink, white, and pale blue—but especially for this combination, I stick with blue. As summer moves along and the vines creep up to 15 or even 30 feet, the flowering increases in vigor. Both vines have tendrils that twine around whatever is in their path, and both have heart-shaped leaves; it is hard to see where one stops and another begins. Unfortunately, they both reseed with abandon, as if working on a massive re-populating scheme. Lately, I've relegated them to the rain chain I hung on the end of the playhouse porch, where they can climb up onto the roof if they like. There is little bare ground nearby for their seeds to sprout.

Before deciding on roses as a permanent solution on the arbor at the orchard's entrance, I grew morning glories there. Then, in the roses' first year, before they were able to make much of an impression, I let morning glories climb up and over them as a sort of transition. By dumb luck, the three repeat-blooming roses and the clematis I also planted there complement each other in sickness and in health (see page 185), and the morning glories are no longer needed.

Clematis 'Duchess of Albany'
(*Clematis* 'Duchess of Albany')

Morning glories
(*Ipomoea tricolor*)

Glematis 'Purpurea Plena Elegans'
(*Clematis viticella* 'Purpurea Plena Elegans')

Clematis 'Duchess of Edinburgh'
(*Clematis* 'Duchess of Edinburgh')

Climbing snapdragon
(*Asarina scandens*)

Hall's honeysuckle
(*Lonicera japonica* 'Halliana')

Clematis 'Vyvyan Pennell'
(*Clematis* 'Vyvyan Pennell')

Clematis
(*Clematis orientalis*)

Cup-and-saucer vine
(*Cobaea scandens*)

Wisteria
(*Wisteria frutescens*)

Perennial Climbers

Perennial vines that sport long limbs and showy flowers—wisteria, honeysuckle, trumpet vine, silver lace vine, cross vine, clematis, climbing hydrangea, and climbing roses—make an impact at a distance.

WISTERIA

Although a newly planted **wisteria** is slow to bloom, it can be overbearing in its later years. It's not unusual to take 7 years' growth to bloom. Its serpentine habit and boa constrictor strength need close watching. The best and most prolific bloom comes when the vine is pruned back monthly during the summer growing season, stopping in September before the following year's flower buds are formed. Pruned as a standard or as a craggy tree, wisteria's undisciplined behavior is kept in check, and its beauty remains flawless.

On our house, pruning wisteria is mandatory several times a year; otherwise, I'll find it growing in an open window or lifting the roof. To play it safe, we attached a wooden beam to the outside of our house, below the second-story windows, to hold two wisterias, one on each side. One mild winter day, after the vines had grown for a few years and were still flexible, we detached the long, 12-foot stems from the house, laid them on the ground, and removed the weak, thin stems, leaving three main stems on each vine. We pruned away the lower leaves up to 8 feet high in order to train the vines to branch above the porch at the second story. Then we braided the main stems, just as I used to braid my daughter's hair. It took two of us to do it, a May dance of sorts, as we stepped up and over one stem and crawled under another while holding on to a third. When we finished, we lifted the braided stems up and retied them to the beam. We clip any sideshoots along the braided section whenever they appear in order to keep the lines of the braids clean up to the beam. As the years have passed, the braid has increased in girth, and the foliage and flowers swag from the beam under the windows as we intended. In late May, while the wisteria hangs in lacy awnings over the upstairs' windows, I always crack the windows and cut a few pendulous blooms to scent the house with their sweet, pervasive perfume.

HONEYSUCKLE

In summer **Hall's honeysuckle** (*Lonicera japonica* 'Halliana') wreathes our front door, tossing long sprays of slender, tubular flowers into the air. These open at night, emitting an intense fragrance. Every time I pass by, my spirits are lifted by its sweet

breath. Honeysuckle is a show in itself. The perfume attracts night-flying moths, and in the moonlight their pollination dance is a sight to see. They pirouette, flutter, and land on point, doing nature's bidding. Once pollinated, the honeysuckle blooms change from white to yellow. Because there are always new flowers opening, the vine is a patchwork of yellow and white flowers all summer long with scattered blooms into late fall. Although it's a favorite of mine, Hall's honeysuckle is an invasive pest in the South and is banned from sale in many states.

The honeysuckle wreathing our front door has been there for almost a century. When in bloom, its sweet perfume wafts throughout the house and garden.

TRUMPET VINE AND SILVER LACE VINE

I've camouflaged our bare and ugly tennis court fence with an assortment of vines and roses. I started with a pair of vines, **trumpet vine** (*Campsis radicans*) and **silver lace vine** (*Polygonum aubertii*), which I alternated around the fence. I envisioned the orange trumpet flowers blooming in a midsummer haze of white plumes. The vines have cooperated, though they took some time to do so; like wisteria, a trumpet vine waits several years before blooming. The trumpet vine's 2- to 3-inch-long blaring orange trumpets are borne in clusters of 6 to 12 and are favored by hummingbirds (a distraction for the tennis player). Over time they can climb 20 to 30 feet on a rough surface, attaching themselves by ivylike aerial roots that cling to walls and other supports. If grown against a building, they are liable to lift roof shingles if you allow them to grow under the eaves. One traveled up the roof of the carpentry shop, and I haven't noticed any damage yet. I cut it back every few years.

The silver lace vine takes off with the speed of a rocket: Plant it and stand back for the countdown. You can clip its wings any time, though, even cutting it back to the ground yearly, and it will still behave beautifully. It twines around any support without harming it and grows 15 feet in a season, dangling huge, billowing sprays of

white, lacy summer flowers. I once saw it trained as an eyebrow over large garage doors. Garage doors are rarely memorable; these were unforgettable.

I am often told: "For the most pleasing effect in a garden, use restraint." There may be something in this, but when it comes to climbers, the sky's the limit. My tennis court is living proof. Mixed in among the trumpet and silver lace vines, climbing roses bloom on the south side, and chocolate vine (*Akebia quinata*) and bittersweet on the west. (I didn't invite the bittersweet; it was a gift from the roadside, delivered by a bird. I let it stay. Perhaps I'll regret it, but for now, I cut it for wreaths and arrangements.) The chocolate vine is a demonstration of ignorance on my part. I didn't know any better. The flowers are hidden by the foliage, the fragrance is hard to find, and the plant is invasive to boot. Thankfully, it is on the wild side of the court, where people rarely go.

Of course, tennis players don't thank me when they have to remove a ball from the clutches of a thorny rose, and the flowers have predictably ruined my tennis, costing me my concentration. Now balls go flying by me as I am distracted by the colors and textures of the vines weaving through the fence.

CROSS VINE

I again lost all restraint over a period of a dozen years when adding climbers to the stucco walls on either side of the driveway at our entrance to the property. First, I planted an assortment of different ivies, and then because they were so slow-growing, I added two **cross vines** (*Bignonia capreolata*), one on each side, to overlay the ivy with clusters of trumpet blooms in many shades of orange blending to red. Cross vine is a self-clinging climber perfect for covering a cement wall. It is beautiful, long-blooming, and so easygoing that in mild areas it might eventually extend out 60 feet. Although it is a native plant, it is too often overlooked. Sometime over the years, a few each of roses 'Autumn Sunset' and 'New Dawn' were planted on both the front and the back of the wall to keep the flowers coming all summer. Next came golden hops (*Humulus lupulus* 'Aureus'), a sprinter that adds light to the shady backside of the wall and a golden halo to the top of the wall with a few rays of sunshine randomly running down the front. This mixture has worked wonderfully, with the ivy clinging closely to the cement and the flowering vines overlaying the ivy. Aside from composting their roots and pruning the vines off the cement frogs adorning the pillars, I spend very little time tending these vines.

CLEMATIS

I grow **clematis** on the fences around the pool, on the espaliered fence of apple and pear trees by the orchard, and up the bare legs of many a rose. The small-flowered, bell-shaped clematis, such as the bright pink 'Duchess of Albany', is a favorite of mine. I admire their dainty, nodding lantern-shaped flowers. They are long-blooming from summer into fall and will climb from 8 to 12 feet.

The trick to growing clematis is to provide shade and coolness on their roots (a few inches of mulch is perfect) and full to partial sun on their heads. Most of them, especially the large-flowered ones, also love lime, which I frequently forget to give them. Every few years I make amends, sprinkling a cup among their compost, which seems to satisfy them. I have planted 'Duchess of Albany' to climb a shrub rose, a vitex, a lilac, and the espaliered apple and pear fence separating the front lawn from the orchard. In all four places, the vine

ABOVE: On the espaliered fence of apple and pear trees separating the lawn from the orchard, the nodding bells of *Clematis alpina* 'Ruby' are a bright addition. OPPOSITE: Cross vine (*Bignonia capreolata*), golden hops (Humulus lupulus 'Aureus'), and *Rosa* 'Autumn Sunset' line the walls at the entrance and freely intermingle as they climb.

wound its way up, around, and through the host, blooming its head off in the branches.

The allure of clematis is strong indeed. The blossoms open outright like saucers, nod like bells, or sparkle like tiny stars in sizes from a beguiling 1 inch to a striking 8 inches across. Most are well mannered and easy to care for, and if properly planted, they can live for 80 years or longer. But with more than 250 species and more than 1,000 cultivars, the choices are bewildering. Of course, not all of these are readily available, but you see my point.

Clematis are at their best when they are placed to break the garden's monotony in flower borders, hiding the bare legs of a climbing rose, as 'Nelly Moser' does for *R.* 'Mme. Grégoire Staechelin', extending the bed by drawing your eye upward. They will delicately scatter an overlay of flowers over and around their host, gently looping a leaf stem for support as they go. Ever since I discovered that the glorious purpose in life of a clematis is to catch hold of another plant and festoon it with flowers, I have become a matchmaker. Clematis were born to marry off. The double purple clematis 'Vyvyan Pennell' blooms in late spring with fully double flowers on the previous year's growth and again in fall with large single blooms on this year's growth. Thus, she can't be pruned in fall nor in spring so she can festoon *R.* 'Bonica' twice a year. Any cleanup takes place right after her first bloom has past.

A 'Golden Showers' climbing rose bloomed for many years over the entrance to the carriage yard with the rich lavender-blue clematis 'Ramona' covering her bare legs like stockings. Then a major fall storm, the tail of a hurricane, whipped a large cane from the wall, killing the rose. The clematis survived, but though I've replanted the rose, the beauty of the previous pair is yet to be recovered.

CLIMBING HYDRANGEA

Climbing hydrangea (*Hydrangea anomala* subsp. *petiolaris*) is one of the best and most versatile of the woody clinging vines. Its fluffy white flower clusters are each 6 to 8

OPPOSITE: *Clematis* 'Nelly Moser' scrambles up the bottom canes of, *Rosa* 'Mme. Grégoire Staechelin'.

purpose in life of a clematis is to catch hold
become a matchmaker.

These natural athletes scamper down hills, leap over and fences, and do somersaults back down, twisting and inches across. The flowers, like those of shrub hydrangeas, dry on the vine, fading from bright white to honey brown over summer. The leaves are finely toothed, oval, and shiny, and they, too, turn a golden autumn color after frost. And though *petiolaris* loses its leaves in winter, its bared winter skeleton of rigid, reddish brown stems and dried flower heads remains ornamental. Frosted with snow, it is a winter beauty. I admit going years without removing the dried flowers—there is only so much a gardener can do—but when the new leaves sprout in spring, the deadheads disappear anyway.

A climbing hydrangea sends out aerial rootlets—or fastholds—that grab onto brick, stone, or wood without harming the surface. When given the opportunity, it may snake up to 75 feet or more, pressing its stems tightly against the wall and supporting lateral branches that may extend 3 feet out. Usually, it sits for a few years, establishing roots; then it accelerates suddenly. It took 6 years before my 6-foot back garden wall was clothed.

At the same time the hydrangea was covering the outside of the wall, R. 'Buff Beauty' was climbing the inside and a *Clematis orientalis* was shimmying up the inside corner. I never made time to prune, so the hydrangea climbed up one side of the wall, and the rose the other. They met at the top and crossed over, each trailing down the other side. The clematis first twisted up the rose, then reached out for the hydrangea. I don't quite understand why they don't strangle each other. But each seems to know its place.

CLIMBING ROSES

Our breakfast terrace presented a problem. There was no ground for planting, and the stucco wall needed dressing. It occurred to me to plant **climbing roses** in half-whiskey half-barrels, but I worried that they would be too exposed to cold. My worries were needless. The two *Rosa* 'Dortmund', planted one on each side, took 3 years to grow up and arch over the kitchen door. They now bloom continuously from

streams, dangle from cliffs, shimmy up trees, walls, turning gracefully as they go.

early summer to late fall, and their rose hips feed the birds in winter. As a bonus, each spring several birds nest among the canes, and we can watch them coming and going to feed their young. I do prune these two roses each spring and sometimes again in summer so that their shape stands out against the wall.

At the entrance to the grape arbor that runs behind the kitchen garden is a shaded seat curtained with climbing roses. Here *R.* 'New Dawn' mingles with once-a-season bloomer *R.* 'American Pillar'. One of the last roses to flower, 'American Pillar' blooms full-out for a month with cascades of small, deep pink flowers, each with a winking white eye. 'New Dawn' starts a month earlier and continues to bloom quietly all summer, picking up for a major show in fall. A little farther down on the grape arbor, *Rosa* 'Veilchenblau', another once-bloomer, is more interesting than beautiful when covered with clusters of single purple roses.

For 5 years, the large-flowered *R.* 'Mme. Grégoire Staechelin' bloomed on a metal pillar alongside the playhouse before reaching out and over two sides of the

roof. *R*. 'Cecile Brunner', known as the sweetheart rose and a favorite for boutonnieres at the beginning of the last century, climbed up the posts and spread its arms to encompass the porch. It is easily recognized by its small, perfect buds and flowers held well above the foliage in clusters of a dozen or more. Unfortunately, it is a once-bloomer, but it goes on for a good 6 weeks.

My failure to deadhead the climbing roses accounts for one pleasant extra. I am blessed with decorative rose hips in a great variety of sizes, shapes, and colors, from the tiny red pearls on *R. multiflora* to the bright orange bobbles on 'Mme. Grégoire Staechelin'. They are delightful to look at, and many of them last through winter to provide nutritious food for birds.

On the arbor at the orchard's entrance, I planted three repeat-blooming, deliciously fragrant climbing roses and a clematis. The festivities begin in early May, when the blushing pink clusters of single blooms of 'Kathleen' festoon the arbor and reach out across the espaliered fence. A few weeks later, they are joined by the cerise double blooms of 'Zephirine Drouhin'. By mid-June, the velvety large, dark

OPPOSITE: In early April, the arbor into the orchard is bare of greenery or blooms. ABOVE, LEFT: By late May, the three repeat-blooming roses, white 'Kathleen', red 'Don Juan', and pink 'Zephirine Drouhin', begin the show. ABOVE, RIGHT: After the roses' first flush, *Clematis viticella* 'Purpurea Plena Elegans' keeps the bloom going for over a month as the roses gradually return.

red double flowers of 'Don Juan' steal the show. For a time, the magnificent three are blooming together. Once the heat of summer slows them down, their bloom is sparse, but then the small, double, dusky violet flowers of *Clematis viticella* 'Purpurea Plena Elegans' are ready to go. Like a seamstress, it uses running stitches to wind its way up, around, and through the roses, even reaching out onto the espaliered fence alongside. It needs no care; I've clipped its blackened threads only at season's end. As fall approaches, the clematis naps and the roses get a second wind.

All climbers, like wayward children, can stand a bit of guidance.

The advantages to combining different climbers, thereby increasing the volume and length of bloom, are obvious. Unintentionally, I discovered that combining these different classes of roses also helps. 'Don Juan', a hybrid tea climber, is drop-dead gorgeous each spring but is blotched by black spot and mildew each summer. When I grew it alone, it was unsightly. 'Zephirine Drouhin', an old Bourbon rose, also suffers from heat stroke. Neither of them is a vigorous climber. The hybrid musk 'Kathleen', on the other hand, climbs up to and over 15 feet. It lovingly embraces the other two, wrapping them in long, disease-free limbs and hiding their failings. Since 'Kathleen' has taken over, I never see any problems. Besides, the red blossoms of 'Don Juan' and the cerise blossoms of 'Zephirine Drouhin' can be easily spotted peeking through the tangle of canes, and they are what I care about. This compatible threesome has grown together for 15 years.

All climbers, like wayward children, can stand a bit of guidance. I learned to watch them in spring during periods of quick growth to see what they want to do and then work with them. If need be, I loosely tie the stems of nonclinging canes to the structure they are to climb using a soft or elastic material such as string or strips of fabric. Any long limbs left flapping in the breeze can be easily damaged. Sometimes I simply tuck one cane under another or gently bend it through the ivy or trellis. This is easy to do when the canes are young and flexible. After the first few years, once a climber has reached the top of its support or covered a wall, it usually needs very little attention.

OPPOSITE: *Rosa* 'Dortmund' grows up out of half whiskey barrels to arch over our back door. The long canes are held in place by a half-dozen hooks. Once a few canes are secured, the other ones twine around them. It is surprising how few hooks it takes to attach the roses.

Garden decoys and diversionary tactics

There comes a time in every gardener's life when she is caught with her petals down. It happens after a heavy rain, a drought, high winds, or a prolonged vacation. No one wants to admit that it is the norm. When visitors are expected, our gardens should look their best.

Last year, after spending a month away, I returned to find my garden had not taken my absence well. The rainy, hot summer spurred its growth. In short, the weeds were winning the ground war, and plants that normally stood tall, slouched. The problem was I had agreed to open my garden for a tour. At the time I was asked, the garden was flush with flowers and I was puffed with pride. Now, as I looked about, my bubble deflated. The tour was less than a week away, and I needed a quick fix. I wanted to make a good impression.

In trying times like these, a gardener needs boundless energy and limitless imagination. I settled on a strategy of donations, distractions, decoys, and dazzle. Before implementing the four Ds, I needed major cleanup.

Weeding was the easy part. Recent rains assured that the weeds pulled up without a struggle. My stack of chaste-tree branches (*Vitex agnus-castus*), saved after winter pruning, dwindled as I staked the droopy. These sturdy twigs branch like a gardener's hands to cradle bushy plants, push easily into the ground, and can be trimmed to any size. When in place, they are camouflaged by the plant's foliage.

Once these basic chores were completed, I scooped up several dozen hellebore yearlings lurking just under their mother's foliage and another dozen rose of Sharon seedlings that had strayed into the gravel driveway. These I would donate to the visitors. No one thinks poorly of gift givers, do they?

My next challenge was filling in the bare spots with color. Shopping at the local nursery or dividing and moving plants was not an option. I needed more time to assess and plan for that. So I employed my distraction tactics. I moved a few pots of flowering annuals adorning the terrace into the bare spots in the border. I reasoned that if the pot is raised atop an upside-down pot, a brick, or a block of wood, just above the plants around it, it might be taken for a design element.

At the front border where a dianthus had departed, I planted a large, scallop-shell birdbath and, farther back, another standing, blue-glazed one. After I filled them with water and floating flowers, they, too, looked like they belonged. If the blue glaze mistakenly gives the impression that there are more flowers, all the better.

On occasion I bring out a traditional bee skep. It's hollow and looks like a straw beehive or a pointy

Because a garden is a good place to shed inhibitions, I've tried many a foolish thing to prepare for company. A scarecrow sitting on a bench in the formal garden or on the front porch is amusing. I've dressed them in everything from traditional farmer attire to the kids' discarded Halloween costumes. Superwoman is a big hit among the working mothers, the ballerina-turned-garden-fairy appeals to garden club ladies, and my giant football player makes the men feel at home. One thing is for sure, none are easily forgotten.

When the group arrived, I decided to be honest. I explained that the untrimmed honeysuckle over the door and the roses draping over the top of the windows were romantic abandon. They seemed to buy it. I noted that if you didn't let the weeds get to a certain size, it was impossible to see if there were any keepers among them. I pointed out a baby tulip tree and smatterings of columbines, lupines, nigella, and foxgloves seedlings while ignoring the bindweed, dock, and smartweed. When a guest admired my 6-foot-tall ironweed in beautiful bloom and asked where to get it, I graciously offered her seed as no nursery I know sells it. It is a native New York weed.

As the tour ended, I overheard one lady say that she found it refreshing to see a lived-in garden. Too ordered a garden, she stated, lacks charm. Here there was no pressure for perfection, so she felt right at home.

Thank goodness I didn't stoop to spiking the lemonade and bringing out the pink flamingos.

turban. I can place it over a sickly plant, use it to shade a new transplant, or set it as an ornament in an empty spot. Visitors never know the troubles it hides. Placed strategically in the garden, it says that I care about the environment. A point in my favor.

When visitors are expected, I often put a floral foam wreath of flowers around the neck of a garden ornament and transplant blooms strategically.

Garden statuary are great decoys and can be moved about as needed. After trimming dead or diseased foliage out of the border, I tucked in a stone rabbit to play peekaboo. A gaggle of geese marched out from a larger opening.

I've noted if I give visitors something to talk about, it makes a better impression. So I tried to dazzle them with a wreath of sunflowers on the gate and hung a chandelier, dripping with clematis 'Autumn Joy', from a tree over a dining table.

in conclusion

I once toured the garden of a professional photographer and garden writer with a group of amateur gardeners.

The garden was in sorry shape, yet the host so enthusiastically described what we had just missed in bloom and his plans for what was to come that the visitors were enraptured. The group left convinced they had seen a great garden. It was the emperor without his clothes. The power of positive thinking, persuasive marketing, and bragging can't be overestimated.

As anyone who gardens knows, a certain number of things are bound to be wrong at any given time. I've had more than my share of garden failures. No doubt this is partly because I'm impulsive and quick to act on an idea. I've always thought patience is overrated. I am now less certain of that, but I'm still not prepared to give up experimenting. Change in a garden, as in life, is good, even if the causes are storms, drought, deluges, or downpours. The art of gardening is knowing when to fight, when to look the other way, and when to accept defeat.

Despite the minor headaches and setbacks that gardening entails, as Samuel Johnson (no gardener, but a wise man) said, "It is by studying little things that we attain the great art of having as little misery and as much happiness as possible." Gardening, more than most activities, is full of "little things," all of which add up to make each day more interesting than the one before.

Such things inevitably include questionable decisions. For example, some years ago, I went a little crazy planting dwarf mondo grass (*Ophiopogon japonicus* 'Nippon') across the back woodland walk in flowing lines—curves, diamonds, and Xs—as if drawn by a pencil. My geometric designs have thickened, but they have not lost their shape. It was a silly thing to do, some would say laughable, but it does go to show that gardeners will never run out of creative uses for plants. And I now know that if

I wanted to bring the fad for logos or initials into the garden, this is the plant to use.

That's not the only time I've done something to make a garden designer cringe. I don't mind; gardening for me is emotional and, often as not, the heart leads the head. Just last week a designer friend asked in horror, "Suzy, how could you?" when spying the 4-foot-tall juniper that I allowed to sprout from a crevice between two boulders alongside the stream. Its proportions were all wrong for the setting, and a juniper is, of course, too common for a discriminating gardener. I knew all that, but I admired its survivor skills. Sympathy has its place in a garden, too.

I usually start off well, planning on paper, scouring nursery catalogs, blending colors, and following my plans when planting. Where I take a wrong turn is in failing to force my will on the garden, even though I know that when plants are allowed to have their own way, chaos is inevitable.

On the back woodland trail, I planted dwarf mondo grass in geometric designs across the path to break up the monotony of the wood chips.

Of course, some plants do not escape my wrath. The gooseneck loosestrife crowding out the lupines and the chameleon plant smelling like a sewer were quickly banished with no regrets. I am quick to chop off the heads of serious offenders. It is the plants in the wrong place at the wrong time that I hesitate to remove. All too often I return from a nursery with plants that caught my eye without a clue about where to plant them. As a rule I shove the new plants in where others have perished. Over time the planting becomes messy, and like it or not, I find that I have to put some discipline and order back into the border. It is not a pleasant job.

Of course I can learn. One expert criticized my woodland walk because the trees were not pruned to allow a higher ceiling over the plantings. It took a few years for the idea to sink in—but all of a sudden, while walking down the woodland path, I had a claustrophobic feeling. I grabbed a saw and began to limb up the trees.

Sometimes, though, I've found it better to stick to my guns. For example, yet another designer, enchanted by our beautiful view of the sea, emphatically told me to cut down more trees to open up the view from the woodland path. He missed the point. We have views of the sea whenever we choose to sit on the bank, at the large pond, the terrace in the formal garden, or for that matter on the beach itself. The woods are a place of privacy, calm, and tranquility—a cathedral of foliage. I don't want to let the outside world in when I come to the woods for a spiritual uplift—not even the sea.

Another designer begged me to open the horseshoe hedge of holly behind the rose bed in the formal garden, to expose the base of a majestic tree. But the hollies were growing on ground 4 feet higher than the ground at the base of the tree; if I opened the hedge, the garden would no longer be level and the way to the tree would be clearly downhill. Our visions were so far apart that to this day, I can't understand what he saw.

None of these criticisms or opinions has depressed me. I know my garden is basically too personal and too private and gives me too much pleasure. Breathtaking beauty often comes in small and unpredictable packages: two climbers giving each other a leg up, an island of witch hazel blooming above the snow, or *Rosa* 'Bonica' trailing a scarf of clematis. I am happy following my heart. Like the sunflowers, I nod toward the sun and rise early to the songs of the birds. And if my garden owns me more than I own it, fair enough.

Besides, just as there are always ways to mask an ugly fence with a rose or a clematis, there are always ways to make a virtue of awkward features. Is the honeysuckle a shambles, dangling helter-skelter over the door? No, it's "romantically lush." Is the garden seat surrounded by clashing roses? No, it's the "the electric bench"—if you don't get a jolt from the color, you will from the scent. Is the aster 'Harrington's Pink' spreading over the phlox, desperately needing to be divided? No, that's "romantic abandon."

If I can't be a good example, I'll settle for being a beacon of warning. Remember, it's your garden.

The art of gardening is knowing when to fight, when to look the other way, and when to accept defeat.

to all my friends

barbara Winkler, the executive editor at *Family Circle*, took a chance on me more than a decade ago. I wrote my first magazine article for her, and she has continued to teach me how to be a better writer ever since. Many of the ideas in this book developed from articles first written for *Family Circle*.

Ginger Rothe, my editor at *Newsday*, gently nudged me forward, asking all the right questions to encourage me to dig deeper for my stories.

The team at Rodale—Margot Schupf, Nancy Bailey, and Patricia Field—are thoughtful, encouraging, smart, helpful, and cheerful and couldn't be easier to work with. They go the extra yard.

I am grateful to Doug Turshen, the book's designer, who helped me think through the book's concept before I wrote it and then brought the ideas to life with his original design. Nora Negron did a wonderful job assisting Doug.

Early on, Charles Elliot helped me craft the book. My father, Ed Frutig, read all along the way, making helpful suggestions. My assistant, Gina Norgard, sorted through pictures, researched topics on the Internet, and helped me weekly in the garden. My husband, Carter, was pushed into service reading various parts of the manuscript, and he never complained. Robert Geline and Christopher Lukas first called me a down-to-earth gardener. Jose Palacio has over many years built our retaining walls, terraces, arbors, fences, garden furniture, and gazebo. His son, Davy, now works with him. Carlos Valle, equipped with a sunny personality and quick wit, has helped maintain the garden the last few years.

Many horticulturists lent expertise and ideas as well. They include Allan M. Armitage, David Austin, Louis Bauer, Rosalind Creasy, Conni and Jim Cross, Ken Druse, J. Barry Ferguson, Michael Marriott, Anne Raver, and Wayne Winterrowd.

The climbing rose 'Don Juan' has great fragrance and beautiful flowers but it is prone to black spot. I grow it with other climbers that hide its leaves so I can still enjoy its flowers.

bibliography

Armitage, Allan M., and Judy M. Laushman. *Specialty Cut Flowers.* Portland, OR: Varsity Press/Timber Press, 2003. *A textbook for cut-flower growers*

———. *Herbaceous Perennial Plants.* Champaign, IL: Stipes Publishing Company, 1989. *A chatty, highly readable, and comprehensive book about perennials by one of America's most respected experts*

Austin, David. *Old Roses and English Roses.* Woodbridge, Suffolk, U.K.: Antique Collectors' Club Ltd., 1993.

Brown, Deni. *The Herb Society of America Encyclopedia of Herbs and Their Uses.* London: Dorling Kindersley Ltd., 1995 (revised 2001).

Bryan, John E. *Bulbs.* Portland, OR: Timber Press, 1989 (revised 2002).

Dirr, Michael A. *Manual of Woody Landscape Plants.* Fifth edition. Champaign, IL: Stipes Publishing Company, 1998.

Druse, Ken. *Making More Plants—The Science, Art, and Joy of Propagation.* New York: Clarkson Potter, 2000.

Ferguson, J. Barry, and Tom Cowan. *Living with Flowers.* New York: Rizzoli International Publications, Inc., 1990 (revised and updated 2003). *Beautifully illustrated and packed with helpful flower-arranging tips*

Fiala, Father John L. *Lilac, The Genus Syringa.* Portland, OR: Timber Press, 1988. *The definitive book on lilacs and highly recommended for lilac lovers*

Genders, Roy. *The Cottage Garden and the Old-Fashioned Flowers.* London: Pelham Books Ltd., 1969.

Lloyd, Christopher. *The Well-Tempered Garden.* London: Penguin Books, 1985. *Every book by Christopher Lloyd is worth reading.*

Johnson, A. T. *A Woodland Garden.* New York: The Lyons Press, 1999.

Poor, Janet Meakin, and Nancy Peterson Brewster, editors. *Plants That Merit Attention.* Vol. II Shrubs. The Garden Club of America. Portland, OR: Timber Press, 1996.

Reddell, Rayford Clayton. *Growing Good Roses.* New York: HarperCollins, 1988.

———. *The Rose Bible.* San Francisco: Chronicle Books, 1998.

Roth, Susan A., and Dennis Schrader. *Hot Plants for Cool Climates.* Boston: Houghton Mifflin, 2000.

Winterrowd, Wayne. *Annuals for Connoisseurs.* New York: Hungry Minds, 1999. *The best book I've read about annuals by a wonderful and insightful gardener*

index

Boldface page references indicate photographs.

C

P

Pachysandra, in wreath, **125**
Pachysandra terminalis 'Silver Edge', 161
Palacio
    Davy, 194
    Jose, 194
Pansies, 9
    as groundcover, **158–159**
Papaver, seeds of, 22–23
Papaver rhoeas, 45
    sowing, 43
Paths. *See also* Lilac and peony walk
    in kitchen garden, **32–33,** 34, **45**
    primrose, 71, 72, **73**
    in woodland walk, **v, 54–55, 80–81, 86–87,** 94,
        191
Peas
    garden (edible)
        sowing, 43
    sweet, 44–45, **44**
        sowing, 43
Penstemon, creeping, 160
Peonies, **146–147, 150, 152**
    'Baroness Schröder', 148
    fall foliage of, 26, **27**
    'Festiva Maxima', **31,** 148
    tree, 140, 148–50, **148**
        'Guardian of the Monastery', 149–50
        'Hephestos', 149–50
Perennials
    drought and, 153
    in formal gardens, 106, **107,** 108–9
    invasive, 7–8
    self-seeding, 18–19, **19, 20,** 21
    in winter, 26, **29**
Periwinkle, 161
Petasites japonicus, **5**
Phaseolus coccineus, 50
Pieris japonica, 95
Pinks, **102, 107**
Planters, **40, 186**
Plant labels, 94
Plant protectors, garden blankets, 43–44, **43**
Plant supports, 104
    chaste tree *(Vitex)* branches as, **50,** 51, 105–6, 188
    roses as, 14
Platycodon grandiflorus, **111**
Plumbago, 164
Podophyllum peltatum, 77
Poison ivy, **5**
Polygonatum odoratum 'Variegtum', **xviii**

Polygonum aubertii, 177, 178
Ponds, **xvi, 57**
Poppies
    Oriental, **107**
    red, 15
    seeds of, 22–23
    Shirley, **23,** 45
        sowing, 23, 43
Porcelain vine, variegated, xi
Porch, **ix**
Potatoes, 46
    'All Blue', 46
    'German Butterball', 46
    planting, 43
    'Yellow Finn', 46
Primroses, **61,** 71–72, **73, 75,** 76
    candelabra, 72
    dividing, **73**
    Japanese, 72
Primula, 71–72, **73,** 76
Primula japonica, 72
Primula 'Mark Viette', 76
Primula veris, 72, **73**
Primula veris 'J. Barry Ferguson', **73,** 76
Pulmonaria angustifolia, 76
Pulmonaria saccarata 'Mrs. Moon', **75**
Puschkinia, 61
Puschkinia scilloides, 61

R

Raver, Anne, 152
Rhododendron yakushimanum, 95
Rosa glauca, 132, **133,** 151–52
Rosa multiflora, 185
Rosa mundi, **127,** 132
Rosa rugosa, **121**
Rosa rugosa rubra, 132–33
Rose garden, formal, **122–123, 129, 130, 133**
    embankment in, 132–33, **133**
    evolution of, 120–21
Rose-of-Sharon, 21, **139**
    'Diana', 140
Rose *(Rosa),* **36–37, 129,** 172. *See also* Roses
    'Abraham Darby', **118–119, 122–123, 126,** 130
    'Aloha', **38, 39, 167**
    'American Pillar', 108, **109, 133, 142, 143,** 184
    'Autumn Sunset', **178**
    'Ballerina', **126,** 132
    'Belinda', 132
    'Blaze', 40
    'Bonica', **126,** 132, **133, 171**

S

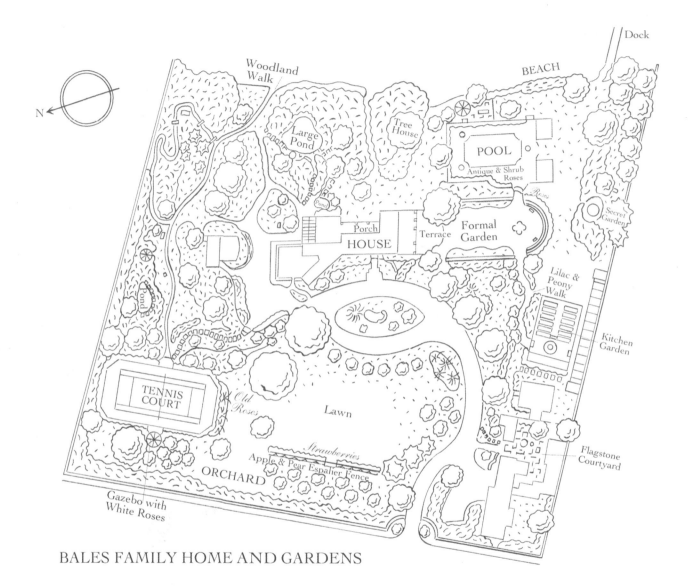

N

Dock

BEACH

Woodland Walk

Large Pond

Tree House

POOL

Antique & Shrub Roses

Roses

Secret Garden

Pond

Porch

HOUSE

Terrace

Formal Garden

Lilac & Peony Walk

Kitchen Garden

Pond

Flagstone Courtyard

TENNIS COURT

Old Roses

Lawn

Strawberries

Apple & Pear Espalier Fence

ORCHARD

Gazebo with White Roses

BALES FAMILY HOME AND GARDENS

THE KITCHEN GARDEN

Morning Glories

Annuals
Perennials
Biennials

Rose

Vegetables

Climbing
Sweet
Peas

Vitex
fence

Cutting
Flowers
Zinnias

Cutting
Flowers

Wood Chips

Salad Greens   Nasturtiums

'The Fairy' Rose

Sunflowers

Cutting
Flowers
Cosmos

Dahlias

whiskey
barrel

Tomatoes

Climbing
Vines

Cutting
Flowers

Rose

Picket Fence   Peas   Peas